VACATION GUIDE TO OAXACA, MEXICO 2024-2025

"Discover the Rich weaves of Oaxaca: Hiking, biking, Trekking, beaches, adventure, A Comprehensive Vacation Guide for 2024-2025"

JOY KIM

DEDICATION

THIS BOOK IS DEDICATED TO ALL THE ADVENTUROUS
TRAVELLERS

CONTENTS

Conclusion

Introduction: Discovering the Enchanting Allure of Oaxaca in 2024-2025

Travelers are drawn to Oaxaca, which is tucked away in the heart of southern Mexico, by its fascinating history, lively culture, and stunning scenery. We'll dive into Oaxaca's spirit as we set off on this virtual adventure, discovering the fascinating fusion of traditional and contemporary elements that make this region unique. We'll discover the factors that make Oaxaca a standout travel destination in 2024–2025 in this in-depth guide.

Overview of Oaxaca

Historical weaves

Oaxaca is proud of its historical fabric, which is weaved from the strands of long-gone civilizations. The terrain is dotted with the ruins of the Zapotec and Mixtec civilizations, and pre-Columbian sites such as Monte Albán and Mitla provide insight into the area's history. Oaxaca City's architecture reflects the colonial influence, which enhances the story of this historic sanctuary.

Cultural Mosaic

Oaxaca's cultural variety is one of its most distinctive qualities. The region's dynamic patchwork is enriched by the distinct customs and languages of its indigenous groups. Markets throughout the city, including Mercado Benito Juarez, highlight this diversity with a rainbow of hues, scents, and handicrafts.

Cuisines

Oaxacan food is evidence of the region's culinary excellence. International praise has been showered upon Oaxacan foods such as mole, tlayudas, and chapulines, which are famous for their intricate flavors and age-old methods. Even the pickiest foodies will find the family-run restaurants and bustling food markets to offer a genuine culinary experience that will tempt their palates.

Natural Splendors

Beyond its traditional charm, Oaxaca is known for its breathtaking natural beauty. The regions varied and scenic landscapes are influenced by the eerie rock formations of Hierve el Agua, the expansive vistas from Monte Albán, and the immaculate beaches along the Oaxacan coast.

Why Visit Oaxaca in 2024-2025

Time-Tested Traditions and Modern Charms

Oaxaca manages to embrace modernity while maintaining its long-standing customs in a careful balance. This balance is more fascinating than ever in 2024–2025. You can observe indigenous craftspeople making elaborate items with methods that have been passed down through the years as you stroll around Oaxaca City's cobblestone streets. Modern art galleries and colorful street art both show how much the area embraces current artistic expression.

Festivals and Celebrations

A variety of festivals and celebrations showcasing Oaxaca's festive spirit are scheduled for the year 2024–2025. The highlight is the internationally recognized Guelaguetza Festival, which honors indigenous music, dancing, and culture. In addition, Oaxaca's Day of the Dead celebrations are a once-in-a-lifetime experience, with the streets a riot of color, ornate altars, and a deep sense of respect for loved ones who have passed away.

Sustainable and Responsible Tourism

Initiatives aimed at promoting responsible and sustainable tourism have Oaxaca at their forefront. In 2024–2025, the area will still place a high priority on cultural preservation, community involvement, and environmentally beneficial methods. By taking part in community-based tourism initiatives, visitors may help preserve Oaxaca's distinctive natural and cultural legacy while also supporting local artists.

Culinary Experiences beyond Compare

Oaxaca is a constantly-evolving gastronomic haven for food lovers. It is anticipated that forward-thinking chefs will combine global influences with native Oaxacan flavors in the upcoming years to create a gastronomic landscape that honors the region's culinary heritage while pushing culinary frontiers. Oaxaca's food sector is ready to treat the senses to a fascinating culinary adventure, ranging from street food vendors to fine-dining venues.

Untouched Landscapes and Adventure Awaits

While Oaxaca City captivates visitors with its cultural riches, the surrounding scenery calls out to those seeking adventure. Oaxaca offers a wide variety of outdoor activities, including trekking in the stunning mountains, discovering historic sites, and relaxing on immaculate beaches. The area's dedication to sustainable tourism in 2024–2025 guarantees that these natural treasures stay unspoiled and open to future generations.

Conclusion

It is clear from the start of this virtual tour of Oaxaca in 2024–2025 that the area is a lively fabric of culture, history, and scenic beauty. Oaxaca offers a vacation experience that goes beyond the typical, whether your interests lie in fine cuisine, rich cultural experiences, or old archaeological sites. Come along as we explore Oaxaca's subtleties in greater detail, revealing the ageless customs and undiscovered treasures that make this place an appealing option for discriminating tourists.

Getting There: Navigating the Pathways to Oaxaca in 2024-2025

Traveling to Oaxaca is an exciting adventure that offers the chance to experience natural beauty and cultural discovery. We'll examine the several routes that lead to Oaxaca in this extensive guide, providing in-depth analyses of available modes of transportation, advice for drivers, and crucial details on entry and visa procedures.

Transportation Options

Air Travel

Oaxaca International Airport (IATA: OAX, ICAO: MMOX)

The main air travel gateway is Oaxaca International Airport, which is tucked away in the mountains. The airport, which is around 7 kilometers (4.3 miles) from Oaxaca City, serves both domestic and international travel. Oaxaca is connected to major cities in Mexico, the United States, and other countries by airlines like Aeroméxico, Volaris, and Interjet.

Ground Transportation from the Airport

Upon arrival, taxis, private shuttles, or rental automobiles from the airport provide easy access to the city center for visitors. The voyage offers a preview of the stunning scenery of Oaxaca, preparing the traveler for the experiences to come.

Bus Services

Central de Autobuses de Oaxaca (CADO)

Long-distance bus travel is a great alternative for individuals looking for something affordable and scenic. The main bus terminal linking Oaxaca with other Mexican towns is called the Central de Autobuses de Oaxaca (CADO). Executive and deluxe class buses have air conditioning, comfy seating, and lavatories to ensure a comfortable ride.

Popular Bus Companies

- ADO (Autobuses de Oriente)
- Estrella de Oro
- OCC (Ómnibus Cristóbal Colón)

Regional and Local Bus Services

In addition to long-distance travel, Oaxaca has a vast local and regional bus network that makes it easy to go around and visit neighboring towns and sites.

Driving Tips

Renting a Car

Those who want to discover Oaxaca at their own pace and with flexibility should consider renting a car. Large automobile rental firms operate in the city center and at the airport, providing a variety of vehicles to suit different needs.

Driving Conditions

Even though Oaxaca's road system has recently undergone improvement, it's important to be aware of the different road conditions. Unpaved roads can exist in some remote locations, therefore a reliable vehicle is necessary for exploration. To guarantee a safe travel, it's also important to abide by local traffic laws and signage.

Scenic Routes

Oaxaca is well known for its beautiful highways, such as the Oaxaca Coast Highway, which offers breath-taking vistas of the Pacific. It is advised that when planning a route, drivers take into account the surrounding scenery as well as any cultural sites.

Visa and Entry Requirements

Tourist Visas

For numerous tourists, obtaining a tourist visa is essential to discovering Oaxaca's hidden gems. Without a visa, citizens of the United States, Canada, the European Union, Australia, and many other nations are able to travel to Mexico. But it's crucial to confirm the precise visa requirements according to your country of origin.

Visitor's Permit (FMM)

Entry by Land

The entry procedures should also be known by anyone traveling to Mexico by land, whether they are driving from the United States or crossing the border. It is advisable to get the necessary documentation in advance of any research that may be required for vehicle permits.

Conclusion

Journey is just as important as destination in 2024–2025 when exploring Oaxaca's beauties. Take a helicopter ride, take a bus across the countryside, or drive a rental car around the city to experience a different side of Oaxaca's allure. We establish the foundation for a vacation that promises natural discovery, cultural immersion, and a smooth transition into the heart of this captivating region as we investigate the logistics of traveling to Oaxaca. So grab a seat, and get ready for an extraordinary voyage that will take you to Oaxaca's natural beauty and rich cultural legacy.

Air Travel Routes

To facilitate your journey, let's explore some recommended air travel routes to Oaxaca:

- **Route 1: International Arrival**
  o Departure City: [Origin City]
  o Arrival City: Oaxaca International Airport (OAX)
  o Airlines: Aeroméxico, Volaris, Interjet
  o Flight Duration: varies
  o Notable Cities En Route: [Connecting City 1], [Connecting City 2]
- **Route 2: Domestic Connection**
  o Departure City: [Origin City within Mexico]
  o Arrival City: Oaxaca International Airport (OAX)
  o Airlines: ADO, Estrella de Oro, OCC
  o Bus Duration: varies
  o Notable Cities En Route: [Connecting City 1], [Connecting City 2]

Bus Travel Routes

Due to its central location in Mexico, Oaxaca can be reached by bus from a number of different cities. These are a few well-traveled paths:

- **Route 1: Mexico City to Oaxaca**
  o Departure: Terminal de Autobuses de Pasajeros de Oriente (TAPO)
  o Arrival: Central de Autobuses de Oaxaca (CADO)
  o Bus Companies: ADO, Estrella de Oro
  o Travel Time: varies
- **Route 2: Puebla to Oaxaca**
  o Departure: Estrella Roja Terminal CAPU
  o Arrival: Central de Autobuses de Oaxaca (CADO)
  o Bus Companies: ADO, Estrella Roja
  o Travel Time: varied

Driving Routes and Maps

Here are two suggested driving routes for people who choose to take the scenic journey by car:

- **Route 1: Mexico City to Oaxaca**
  - Departure: [Starting Point in Mexico City]
  - Arrival: Oaxaca City
  - Distance: varied
  - Estimated Drive Time: varied
  - Highlights: [Scenic Stops and Attractions]
- **Route 2: Oaxaca Coastal Drive**
  - Departure: Oaxaca City
  - Arrival: Puerto Escondido
  - Distance: varied
  - Estimated Drive Time: varied
  - Highlights: [Coastal Towns, Beaches, and Natural Attractions]

Practical Maps and Coordinates

To assist in your journey, here are key locations with longitude and latitude coordinates:

- **Oaxaca International Airport (OAX)**
  - Latitude: 17.0008° N
  - Longitude: 96.7221° W
- **Central de Autobuses de Oaxaca (CADO)**
  - Latitude: *17.0654 N*
  - Longitude: *-96.7237 W*
- **Oaxaca City Center**
  - Latitude: 17.0732° N
  - Longitude: 96.7266° W
- **Hierve el Agua**
  - Latitude: 16.8657° N
  - Longitude: 96.2760° W
- **Monte Albán Archaeological Site**
  - Latitude: 17.0466° N

     o   Longitude: 96.7659° W

Utilizing these coordinates with mapping applications or navigation systems will guarantee a convenient and pleasurable travel experience.

Visa and Entry Requirements Checklist

Make sure you have the following before you travel to Oaxaca:

1. **Passport:** Valid for at least six months beyond your planned departure from Mexico.
2. **Tourist Visa:** Not required for citizens of [Your Country]. Verify the particular requirements according to your country of origin.
3. **Visitor's Permit (FMM):** Obtain and fill out the FMM form upon arrival in Mexico.
4. **Land Entry Documentation:** If entering Mexico by land, research and obtain any necessary permits or documents for your vehicle.
5. **Travel Insurance:** Consider purchasing travel insurance to cover unforeseen circumstances during your journey.

By taking into account these routes and making sure you have all the required paperwork, you'll be set up for a smooth and enjoyable journey to Oaxaca in 2024–2025. Traveling to Oaxaca may be as exciting as the destination itself, whether you're taking a road trip, flying through the air, or riding a bus.

Additional Travel Tips

Language and Communication

Even though Oaxaca and all of Mexico use Spanish as their official language, you can still hear some English spoken in tourist areas. Acquiring a few fundamental Spanish phrases might improve your encounters and communication with native speakers. Pocket phrasebooks and language apps make great travel companions.

Currency and Money Matters

The Mexican Peso (MXN) is the national currency of Mexico. In Oaxaca City, ATMs are widely dispersed and offer a practical means of withdrawing local cash. Most hotels, restaurants, and larger establishments take credit cards, but in more isolated places and for smaller purchases, it's best to have some cash on hand.

Health and Safety

Consult your healthcare practitioner about necessary immunizations prior to your trip to Oaxaca. A simple first aid kit and any required prescription drugs should also be carried. Travelers can feel comfortable in Oaxaca, but like with any place, it's important to remain alert and aware of your surroundings.

Local Transportation

Oaxaca City has a well-developed cab and local bus network, making transportation around the city reasonably simple. Walking is a fantastic method to discover the city's lovely streets across short distances. There are local buses, guided tours, and rental automobiles if you want to explore the nearby areas.

Weather Considerations

The climate of Oaxaca is not uniform; the coastal regions have a more tropical environment, while the upland areas have a more temperate climate. Make sure you pack for the weather on the days you have selected by checking the forecast. Wearing comfortable clothing, a hat, and sunscreen is vital, particularly if you intend to visit outdoor attractions.

Suggested Itineraries

Take into consideration the following suggested itineraries to make the most of your time in Oaxaca:

One Week in Oaxaca: Cultural Immersion and Nature Exploration

- **Day 1-3: Oaxaca City**
- Take in the Oaxacan cuisine, tour museums, and stroll around the ancient city center.
- Visit regional markets to take in the lively atmosphere.
- **Day 4-5: Monte Albán and Surroundings**
- Explore Monte Albán, an old archaeological site.
- See neighboring towns that are known for their traditional crafts.
- **Day 6-7: Hierve el Agua and Oaxacan Coast**

See Hierve el Agua's petrified waterfalls.

Unwind on the beaches in Mazunte or Puerto Escondido.

Extended Stay Recommendations: Diving Deeper into Oaxacan Culture

- **Week 1-2: Language and Cooking Classes**
- Encounter Oaxacan culture by enrolling in language classes.
- Take cooking classes to become an expert in Oaxacan cooking.
- **Week 3-4: Community-Based Tourism and Volunteering**
    - Take part in projects promoting community-based tourism.
    - Look into volunteer possibilities to support neighborhood initiatives.

Conclusion

Armed with knowledge on travel, obtaining a visa, and useful advice, you're ready to explore Oaxaca in 2024–2025, a place that effortlessly combines historic customs with contemporary attractiveness. The warmth of its people, the depth of its culture, and the tastes of its food are all part of Oaxaca's attraction, in addition to its beautiful scenery. Whatever your interests—history, outdoor activities, or cuisine—Oaxaca extends a warm welcome and promises an enlightening and remarkable journey. I hope your journey to Oaxaca along the roads is as colorful and engrossing as the cultural mosaic that this treasure from Mexico has to offer. Happy travels!

Accommodations in Oaxaca: A Comprehensive Guide for Every Traveler in 2024-2025

Introduction to Oaxacan Hospitality

One of the most important things to think about when planning your trip to the fascinating city of Oaxaca in 2024–2025 is selecting the ideal lodging. There is a wide variety of hotels available in Oaxaca to suit different tastes and price ranges. With opulent hotels that radiate elegance and quaint boutique inns that encapsulate the spirit of the region, this guide will help you make your way through Oaxaca's lodging options.

Hotels in Oaxaca

Luxury Hotels

Quinta Real Oaxaca

- *Address:* Calle 5 de Mayo #300, Centro, 68000 Oaxaca de Juárez, Oax., Mexico
- *Latitude:* [17.0636° N]
- *Longitude:* [96.7271° W]

Quinta Real Oaxaca is an oasis of sophistication and tranquility in the heart of Oaxaca City. Housed in a former 16th-century convent, this luxury hotel seamlessly blends colonial architecture with modern amenities. The lush courtyard, exquisite dining options, and opulent rooms make it an ideal choice for those seeking a refined stay.

Hotel Azul

- *Address:* Calle Abasolo 313, Col. Centro, Oaxaca City, Mexico
- *Latitude:* [17.0602° N]
- *Longitude:* [96.7225° W]

Hotel Azul offers modern comfort with a dash of creative flair close to the busy Zócalo. A local artist has created a distinctive design for each room, resulting in a lively and colorful ambiance. The rooftop patio is the ideal place to unwind because it offers breathtaking city views.

Casa Oaxaca El Restaurante Hotel

- *Address:* Constitución 104, Centro Histórico, 68000 Oaxaca de Juárez, Oax., Mexico
- *Latitude:* [17.0648° N]
- *Longitude:* [96.7242° W]

Casa Oaxaca is a name that connotes elegance and superb cuisine. The best of Oaxacan food is served in an award-winning restaurant at this boutique hotel, which also has tastefully decorated rooms. Visitors may easily discover the city's cultural treasures because to its central location.

Mid-Range Hotels

Hotel Parador de Alcalá

- *Address:* Armenta y López 215, Centro, 68000 Oaxaca de Juárez, Oax., Mexico
- *Latitude:* [17.0652° N]
- *Longitude:* [96.7279° W]

Tucked away in a structure from the colonial era, Hotel Parador de Alcalá provides an elegant and pleasant getaway without going over budget. With its colorful bougainvillea adorning the courtyard, it offers a tranquil environment and is a great option for mid-range travelers due to its close proximity to key attractions.

Hotel CasAntica

- *Address:* Calle 5 de Mayo #300, Centro, 68000 Oaxaca de Juárez, Oax., Mexico
- *Latitude:* [17.0636° N]
- *Longitude:* [96.7271° W]

The Hotel CasAntica blends the traditional beauty of Oaxaca with contemporary conveniences. There is a nice swimming pool in the courtyard, and the apartments are tastefully decorated. This midrange hotel is well located, has attentive service, and is very good value.

Hotel Marqués del Valle

- *Address:* Miguel Hidalgo 113, Centro, 68000 Oaxaca de Juárez, Oax., Mexico
- *Latitude:* [17.0666° N]
- *Longitude:* [96.7245° W]

The Hotel Marqués del Valle, housed in a magnificently refurbished colonial estate, epitomizes Oaxacan friendliness. Indigenous artwork adorning the courtyard creates a warm and inviting ambiance. Guests may stroll about the city's attractions thanks to the hotel's convenient location.

Budget Hotels

Hotel Trebol

- *Address:* Calzada Madero 215, Centro, 68000 Oaxaca de Juárez, Oax., Mexico
- *Latitude:* [17.0660° N]
- *Longitude:* [96.7248° W]

In the center of Oaxaca City, Hotel Trebol provides basic yet cozy lodging for guests on a tight budget. The hotel's courteous personnel and spotless rooms create a pleasant ambiance, and its reasonable rates let visitors set aside money to spend on sightseeing in the area.

Hotel Rivera del Angel

- *Address:* Abasolo 111, Centro, 68000 Oaxaca de Juárez, Oax., Mexico
- *Latitude:* [17.0629° N]
- *Longitude:* [96.7262° W]

Hotel Rivera del Angel is an inexpensive choice in a handy position, only a short stroll from the Zócalo. Budget-conscious tourists can enjoy the city without sacrificing comfort thanks to the simple yet practical rooms.

Hotel Posada San José

- *Address:* Calzada Madero 217, Centro, 68000 Oaxaca de Juárez, Oax., Mexico
- *Latitude:* [17.0659° N]
- *Longitude:* [96.7248° W]

The Hotel Posada San José provides reasonably priced lodging in a picturesque colonial environment. The hotel's straightforward accommodations offer a convenient starting point for discovering Oaxaca, and its close proximity to major sites makes it an economical option for those on a tight budget.

Boutique Inns and Bed & Breakfasts

La Catrina de Alcalá

- *Address:* Calle 5 de Mayo 307, Centro, 68000 Oaxaca de Juárez, Oax., Mexico
- *Latitude:* [17.0634° N]
- *Longitude:* [96.7279° W]

La Catrina de Alcalá's quaint décor and attentive service perfectly encapsulate Oaxacan culture. Each of the distinctively furnished rooms at this boutique hotel tells a tale about a local custom. Guests may fully immerse themselves in the lively ambiance of the city thanks to the central position.

Casa de las Bugambilias

- *Address:* Reforma 402, Centro, 68000 Oaxaca de Juárez, Oax., Mexico
- *Latitude:* [17.0618° N]
- *Longitude:* [96.7242° W]

The peaceful Casa de las Bugambilias is located in the center of Oaxaca. Housed in a mansion from the colonial era, this bed & breakfast offers elegantly appointed rooms and gorgeous gardens. It's a popular among visitors looking for a special and private stay because of the attentive service and substantial breakfast.

Alternative Accommodations

Airbnb

There are lots of Airbnb choices available in Oaxaca, from comfortable flats in the city center to rustic cottages in the countryside. For more luxury and flexibility, travelers can choose a private residence or go for a homestay experience to fully immerse themselves in the local way of life.

Hostels

Hostels in Oaxaca offer a lively and social atmosphere for travelers on a budget who are also interested toward socializing. Hostels are a great option for single travelers or people trying to meet new people because of its communal rooms and dormitory-style lodgings, which encourage connections amongst visitors.

Conclusion

Selecting the ideal accommodations is essential to creating a trip that will never be forgotten, and Oaxaca offers a wide range of lodging choices to suit every preference and budget. Oaxaca's hospitality guarantees a warm and pleasant stay, regardless of your preference for the elegance of boutique inns, the comfort of mid-range options, the price of budget hotels, or the flexibility of alternative accommodations.

Let your lodging selection in 2024–2025 represent your travel interests as you meander through the streets of Oaxaca. Oaxaca welcomes tourists, offering not only a place to rest but also an essential component of the rich cultural experience that lies ahead. Its attractions range from the luxurious to the charming, the conveniently placed to the hidden treasures. Thus, make yourself at home, enjoy the uniqueness of the area, and watch as Oaxaca's enchantment happens all around you. Have a safe journey and ¡hola an Oaxaca!

Tips for Choosing the Right Accommodation

Define Your Priorities

Decide what your top priorities are before making any accommodations. Knowing your priorities will help you make decisions based on factors like money, desired level of cultural immersion, or accessibility to attractions.

Read Reviews and Ratings

Through user reviews, travel websites such as Booking.com, Airbnb, and TripAdvisor offer insightful information. To make an informed choice, pay attention to comments about the whole experience, cleanliness, and service.

Consider Location

The place you choose might have a big impact on your experience. Staying in Oaxaca City's historic core can be the best option if you're the type that prefers a central hub with easy access to attractions. On the other hand, if you're looking for peace and quiet, a seaside hotel or rural getaway close to Puerto Escondido would be more appropriate.

Embrace Cultural Immersion

A chance for cultural immersion can be found at boutique hotels, bed & breakfasts, and certain Airbnb listings. Your connection to Oaxaca's culture is enhanced by hosts who frequently offer more individualized experiences, share local insights, and suggest hidden gems.

Evaluate Amenities

Consider the attributes that hold the greatest significance for you. Whether it's a communal space at a hostel, a rooftop terrace offering breathtaking views, or a swimming pool, make sure your lodging choice suits your tastes to guarantee a relaxing stay.

Visualizing Oaxaca Accommodations - Maps and Coordinates

Here are some maps and the locations for a few of the accommodations to help you navigate:

Luxury Hotels

- **Quinta Real Oaxaca**
  - *Latitude:* 17.0636° N
  - *Longitude:* 96.7271° W
- **Hotel Azul**
  - *Latitude:* 17.0602° N
  - *Longitude:* 96.7225° W
- **Casa Oaxaca El Restaurante Hotel**

- o *Latitude:* 17.0648° N
- o *Longitude:* 96.7242° W

Mid-Range Hotels

- **Hotel Parador de Alcalá**
  - o *Latitude:* 17.0652° N
  - o *Longitude:* 96.7279° W
- **Hotel CasAntica**
  - o *Latitude:* 17.0636° N
  - o *Longitude:* 96.7271° W
- **Hotel Marqués del Valle**
  - o *Latitude:* 17.0666° N
  - o *Longitude:* 96.7245° W

Budget Hotels

- **Hotel Trebol**
  - o *Latitude:* 17.0660° N
  - o *Longitude:* 96.7248° W
- **Hotel Rivera del Angel**
  - o *Latitude:* 17.0629° N
  - o *Longitude:* 96.7262° W
- **Hotel Posada San José**
  - o *Latitude:* 17.0659° N
  - o *Longitude:* 96.7248° W

Boutique Inns and Bed & Breakfasts

- **La Catrina de Alcalá**
  - o *Latitude:* 17.0634° N
  - o *Longitude:* 96.7279° W
- **Casa de las Bugambilias**
  - o *Latitude:* 17.0618° N
  - o *Longitude:* 96.7242° W

Alternative Accommodations

- **Airbnb and Hostels**
  - ○ Coordinates vary based on individual listings. Refer to the specific address and location details provided by the host or hostel.

Booking Your Stay

After you've decided on your ideal lodging, you might want to make a direct reservation via the hotel's website or the official Airbnb app. This frequently guarantees the greatest prices and offers a direct channel of contact with the business.

Conclusion: Creating Lasting Memories in Oaxaca

The lodging you choose for Oaxaca becomes more than just a place to stay as your journey begins; it becomes a crucial component of the whole experience. Whichever lodging option you choose—the opulent settings of a luxury hotel, the charming atmosphere of a boutique inn, or the cozy comfort of a hostel—it all adds to the fabric of memories you'll make while visiting.

Savor Oaxaca's cultural diversity, mingle with the lively locals, and let your lodging of choice act as a warm retreat for the duration of your travels. With the help of maps, coordinates, and enlightening advice, you'll be well-prepared to make choices that will improve your time in Oaxaca. I hope your lodging is as amazing as the location, and that you have a wonderful time exploring, unwinding, and experiencing the thrill of discovery during your stay in Oaxaca. ¡Welcome to Oaxaca!

Special Considerations for Alternative Accommodations: Airbnb and Hostels

Airbnb Experiences in Oaxaca

The Airbnb platform in Oaxaca provides a diverse range of activities that go beyond standard lodging. Think about going on guided tours, taking cooking classes, or attending artisan workshops with your hosts. An authentic cultural experience and an opportunity to establish a deeper connection with Oaxaca are offered by this tailored approach.

Hostels: Budget-Friendly and Socially Vibrant

Hostels in Oaxaca are great choices for budget-conscious travelers looking for a lively social scene and affordable accommodations. These places frequently plan social events, fostering a community where visitors may exchange tales and make new acquaintances. Hostels are ideal places to meet other tourists and explore the city because of their central positions.

Sustainable Stays in Oaxaca

Oaxaca provides environmentally friendly lodging options as guests' concerns about sustainability grow. Seek out lodging establishments that put an emphasis on eco-friendly initiatives including trash minimization, energy conservation, and community involvement. By booking a sustainable stay, you can lessen your influence on the environment and help to protect Oaxaca's natural and cultural legacy.

Staying Safe and Healthy

Although travel to Oaxaca is generally safe, it's important to put your health first. Select lodgings that offer security features like secure entrances and round-the-clock front desks. Take into account the hygiene and cleanliness standards of the establishment you have selected as well, particularly in light of worldwide health concerns. Several lodging establishments have included improved hygiene practices to guarantee a secure and pleasant visit.

Exploring Oaxaca beyond Your

Accommodation

Your selected accommodation acts as a springboard for exploration, and Oaxaca's varied attractions entice you to go beyond your accommodations. Think about designing a schedule that include stops at:

- **Cultural and Historical Sites:** Discover the historic heart of Oaxaca City, take a leisurely stroll around the ancient ruins of Monte Albán, and visit museums that highlight the rich history of the area.
- **Artisan Markets:** Take in the vivid hues and handicrafts found in neighborhood markets like Mercado 20 de Noviembre and Mercado Benito Juarez.
- **Culinary Adventures:** Savor the widely recognized food of Oaxaca by trying local specialties, going to cooking seminars, and visiting street food markets.
- **Natural Wonders:** Explore the stunning scenery of Hierve el Agua, go hiking in the Sierra Norte highlands, or unwind on Puerto Escondido's immaculate beaches.
- **Festivals and Celebrations:** Look out for celebrations such as the Day of the Dead, Guelaguetza, and other regional occasions that provide an insight into Oaxaca's vibrant cultural environment.

Crafting Unforgettable Memories

Every lodging you choose in Oaxaca adds to the story of your trip, so keep that in mind when you arrange your exploration of this fascinating area. Oaxaca welcomes you with open arms, whether you choose to stay in a five-star hotel, interact with other travelers in a hostel, or find comfort in a small inn.

May the vivid weaves of Oaxaca's culture be framed by your lodging, and may the kindness of its people, the delectable tastes of its food, and the breathtaking scenery of its surroundings enrich your memory. ¡Que tengas una gran vez en Oaxaca durante tu estancia en 2024–2025? (Have fun while visiting Oaxaca!)

Savoring Oaxaca: A Culinary Odyssey in 2024-2025

Introduction to Oaxacan Cuisine

Traveling to Oaxaca offers you more than just an eye-candy experience—it's a culinary excursion that urges you to discover the diverse range of Oaxacan food. This book explores the core of Oaxaca's eating scene, highlighting the must-try dishes, well-liked eateries, and hidden treasures that characterize the region's culinary landscape—from complex flavors to centuries-old culinary traditions.

Oaxacan Cuisines

Mole: A Symphony of Flavors

La Teca

- *Address:* Alcalá 110, Ruta Independencia, 68000 Oaxaca de Juárez, Oax., Mexico
- *Latitude:* 17.0606° N
- *Longitude:* 96.7273° W

A trip through Oaxaca's national dish, mole, is provided by La Teca, a restaurant well known for it. A range of mole variants, such as the sophisticated black mole (mole Negro) and the fragrant yellow mole (mole amarillo), are available on the menu, each with a distinctive blend of ingredients.

El Topil

- *Address:* Calle del 5 de Mayo 205, Ruta Independencia, 68000 Oaxaca de Juárez, Oax., Mexico
- *Latitude:* 17.0607° N
- *Longitude:* 96.7266° W

Tucked away in the historic center, El Topil provides a delicious exploration of the world of moles. The variety of mole variations, served with tender meats or vegetables, demonstrates the richness of Oaxacan culinary creativity.

Tlayudas: Oaxacan Pizza with a Twist

Tlayudas Libres

- *Address:* Calle Miguel Hidalgo 706, Ruta Independencia, 68000 Oaxaca de Juárez, Oax., Mexico
- *Latitude:* 17.0660° N
- *Longitude:* 96.7232° W

Tlayudas Libres is the creator of the famous Oaxacan tlayuda, also known as "Oaxacan pizza." This flavorful dish is made with large, thin tortillas topped with a mixture of refried beans, cabbage, avocados, cheese, and your choice of meats.

Itanoni

- *Address:* Belisario Domínguez 513, Col. Reforma, 68050 Oaxaca de Juárez, Oax., Mexico
- *Latitude:* 17.0552° N
- *Longitude:* 96.7266° W

Nestled in the Reforma district, Itanoni elevates tlayudas to a whole new level with its use of heritage maize varietals. The end product is a tasty and crisp tlayuda that honors Oaxaca's agricultural past.

Tamales: A Pockets of Flavor

Tamales Fina Estampa

- *Address:* Murguía 218, Centro, 68000 Oaxaca de Juárez, Oax., Mexico
- *Latitude:* 17.0653° N
- *Longitude:* 96.7233° W

For authentic Oaxacan tamales, the well-liked location is Tamales Fina Estampa. A popular and cozy Oaxacan cuisine, these tamales are loaded with a variety of ingredients like mole, chicken, or black beans and are steam-cooked to perfection.

Tamalería El Chabelo

- *Address:* Calle Armenta y López 801, Ruta Independencia, 68000 Oaxaca de Juárez, Oax., Mexico
- *Latitude:* 17.0595° N
- *Longitude:* 96.7265° W

Famous for its wide selection of tamales, Tamalería El Chabelo offers both savory and sweet options. Tourists may savor tamales that are wrapped in banana leaves and packed with flavors that highlight Oaxaca's diverse culinary heritage.

Must-Try Dishes and Drinks

Chapulines: Crunchy Delicacies

Mercado Benito Juarez

- *Address:* Calle Las Casas 712, Col. Reforma, 68050 Oaxaca de Juárez, Oax., Mexico
- *Latitude:* 17.0645° N
- *Longitude:* 96.7281° W

Mercado Benito Juarez is the ideal location for foodies with a bold palate to try chapulines, which are crispy grasshoppers flavored with garlic, lime, and chili. This protein-rich snack from Oaxaca offers a distinctive twist to the culinary experience.

Tacos de Canasta: Portable Pleasures

Tacos Pehua

- *Address:* Porfirio Díaz 203, Centro, 68000 Oaxaca de Juárez, Oax., Mexico
- *Latitude:* 17.0658° N
- *Longitude:* 96.7234° W

Basket tacos, also known as tacos de Canasta, are a common street snack. These tender, steaming tacos from Tacos Pehua are excellent when stuffed with a range of ingredients, including as potatoes, chorizo, and beans. These tasty and convenient treats are ideal for a quick and satisfying snack.

Oaxacan Mezcal: Liquid Gold

Mezcaloteca

- *Address:* Reforma 506, Centro, 68000 Oaxaca de Juárez, Oax., Mexico
- *Latitude:* 17.0613° N
- *Longitude:* 96.7240° W

A trip to Oaxaca wouldn't be complete without sampling its famous mezcal. Mezcaloteca is an immersive experience that lets guests sample several iterations of this handcrafted alcoholic beverage and learn about its cultural significance and manufacturing methods.

In Situ Mezcalería

- *Address:* Callejón de la Igualdad 100, Col. Reforma, 68050 Oaxaca de Juárez, Oax., Mexico
- *Latitude:* 17.0587° N
- *Longitude:* 96.7258° W

A comfortable setting is offered by In Situ Mezcalería for enjoying a large assortment of mezcal. Experienced staff members provide guests with a remarkable mezcal tasting by guiding them through the subtle differences between each variety.

Popular Restaurants and Street Food

Gourmand's Paradise: Calle Alcalá

Pitiona

- *Address:* Calle de Ignacio Allende 114, Ruta Independencia, 68000 Oaxaca de Juárez, Oax., Mexico
- *Latitude:* 17.0610° N
- *Longitude:* 96.7265° W

Pitiona is a true culinary gem, and Calle Alcalá is a gourmet heaven. Pitiona, a restaurant known for its creative take on traditional Oaxacan food, has a menu that skillfully combines flavors and textures to provide a memorable dining experience.

Street Food Extravaganza: Mercado 20 de Noviembre

Tlayudas el Negro

- *Address:* Mercado 20 de Noviembre, Calle 20 de Noviembre, Col. Ruta Independencia, 68000 Oaxaca de Juárez, Oax., Mexico
- *Latitude:* 17.0641° N
- *Longitude:* 96.7223° W

The aroma of grilled meats and spices permeates the lively Mercado 20 de Noviembre marketplace. Popular restaurant Tlayudas el Negro serves delicious tacos, empanadas, and tlayudas among other street food treats.

Tradition Meets Elegance: Restaurante Los Danzantes

Restaurante Los Danzantes

- *Address:* Macedonio Alcalá 403, Ruta Independencia, 68000 Oaxaca de Juárez, Oax., Mexico
- *Latitude:* 17.0604° N
- *Longitude:* 96.7275° W

In Oaxaca, Restaurante Los Danzantes is the epitome of fine dining. A classy dining experience is provided by the restaurant's ambiance and menu, which honor traditional ingredients. For those looking for a fusion of elegance and tradition, Los Danzantes is a must-visit, serving masterfully made cuisine and handcrafted beverages.

Conclusion: A Culinary Odyssey in Oaxaca

Let your taste buds lead the way as you explore Oaxaca's bustling streets in 2024–2025. Oaxacan food is a celebration of culture, tradition, and the complex artistry of flavors rather than merely eating. Every culinary experience adds a layer to the rich weaves of Oaxaca's gastronomic heritage, from the vibrant markets to the sophisticated elegance of top-notch restaurants.

Remember that every item you enjoy, including mole, tlayudas, and mezcal, conveys a tale about the indigenous origins of Oaxaca, its abundant agriculture, and the inventiveness of its people. I hope you have a lovely culinary adventure in Oaxaca that is full of strong flavors, unexpected delights, and the hospitality of people who are proud to share their culinary secrets with you. Cheers to your success! (Enjoy your food!)

Culinary Exploration Beyond Oaxaca City

Coastal Delights in Puerto Escondido

El Cafecito

- *Address:* Zicatela, Puerto Escondido, Oax., Mexico
- *Latitude:* 15.8700° N
- *Longitude:* 97.0693° W

Visit Puerto Escondido for a taste of the coast's cuisine. Located in the Zicatela neighborhood, El Cafecito serves up fresh catches cooked in traditional Oaxacan ways, making for a seafood feast. Savor shrimp cocktails, grilled seafood, and ceviche while taking in the sea wind.

La Olita

- *Address:* Blvd. Benito Juárez, Zicatela, Puerto Escondido, Oax., Mexico
- *Latitude:* 15.8571° N
- *Longitude:* 97.0646° W

Enjoy the catch of the day at La Olita, a restaurant by the ocean. This restaurant offers seafood platters and whole grilled fish, perfectly encapsulating the spirit of coastal Oaxacan cuisine. Enjoy a refreshing cerveza with your lunch and take in the sun-kissed atmosphere.

Mountain Flavors in the Sierra Norte

Comedor Oaxaqueño

- *Address:* San Juan Atepec, Ixtlán de Juárez, Oax., Mexico
- *Latitude:* 17.2566° N
- *Longitude:* 96.3473° W

In the Sierra Norte region, visit Comedor Oaxaqueño to experience the flavors of mountainous Oaxacan cuisine. Authentically tasting Oaxaca's highland culinary traditions, this rustic eatery is known for its robust stews, earthy tastes, and locally produced ingredients.

Restaurante Tierra Antigua

- *Address:* Reforma, Ixtlán de Juárez, Oax., Mexico
- *Latitude:* 17.2722° N
- *Longitude:* 96.2997° W

Nestled in Ixtlán de Juárez's magnificent settings lies Restaurante Tierra Antigua. The menu offers a distinctive culinary perspective influenced by the region's hilly terrain, including dishes inspired by indigenous Zapotec cuisine.

Culinary Festivals and Events

Guelaguetza: The Festival of Sharing

Known as "Oaxaca's most beautiful festival," the Guelaguetza honors the customs and cultures of the indigenous people. Every year in July, it's a colorful exhibition of dancing, music, and food. The smells of mole, tamales, and tlayudas fill the marketplaces and streets, creating a multisensory experience that highlights the variety of Oaxacan food.

Day of the Dead: Culinary Offerings for Ancestral Spirits

In early November, Oaxacans honor their ancestors with ornate altars decorated with customary dishes during the Day of the Dead ceremonies. Among the food items offered in remembrance of the deceased are mole, sugar skulls, and pan de muerto. Discover the importance of food in this deeply ingrained festivity by strolling around the marketplaces and streets.

Culinary Workshops and Experiences

Seasons of My Heart Cooking School

- *Address:* Etla, Oax., Mexico

- *Latitude:* 17.2057° N
- *Longitude:* 96.8182° W

Encounter the rich culinary customs of Oaxaca by taking part in a cooking class. The charming hamlet of Etla is home to the hands-on Seasons of My Heart Cooking School, where you can learn how to make traditional cuisine under the direction of skilled chefs.

La Cocina Oaxaqueña

- *Address:* Trujano 22, Centro, 68000 Oaxaca de Juárez, Oax., Mexico
- *Latitude:* 17.0610° N
- *Longitude:* 96.7219° W

Located in the center of Oaxaca City, La Cocina Oaxaqueña offers cooking workshops that explore the nuances of Oaxacan food. These seminars provide an interactive investigation of the culinary traditions of the region, including topics such as perfecting the art of mole and creating flawless tlayudas.

Conclusion: A Feast for the Senses

The cuisine of Oaxaca is a colorful weaves woven with regional specialties, customs, and folklore. Recall that every mouthful is an exploration of the core of Oaxacan culture as you stroll through the busy marketplaces, eat in classy restaurants, and indulge in delicious street cuisine.

Enjoying seafood by the sea, sipping mezcal in the highlands, or indulging in Oaxaca City's many offerings—each gastronomic encounter is an ode to the region's rich cultural diversity. May your senses be aroused, your taste buds thrilled, and your memories flavored with the essence of Oaxacan cuisine as you set off on your culinary journey in 2024–2025. ¡Buen provecho y tenga muchos gustos! (Good appetite and have fun!)

Navigating Oaxaca's Culinary Scene: Practical Tips

Exploring Markets and Street Food Safely

The marketplaces of Oaxaca are a veritable gold mine of delicious food, but proceed with caution while visiting. Savor the lively ambiance of markets such as Mercado Benito Juarez and Mercado 20 de Noviembre, but keep your personal possessions and cleanliness in mind. To ensure freshness and safety when enjoying street food, choose vendors with tidy setups and rapid turnover.

Dietary Considerations and Allergies

Although Oaxacan food is very varied, it's important to let people know if you have any dietary needs or allergies when you go out to eat. You can improve your dining experience by knowing certain important phrases in Spanish relating to dietary preferences, as many restaurants and street sellers are flexible.

Embrace the Local Dining Etiquette

Take up the customs of Oaxacan dining to fully immerse yourself in the culture. Before you begin your dinner, it is customary to say "buen provecho" to others. Savor every meal and take pleasure in the companionship of those around you when dining al fresco, since Oaxacans value relaxed dining times.

Mezcal Tasting Etiquette

Enjoy the famous mezcal from Oaxaca, but remember to honor the craft and history that go along with this artisan spirit. During mezcal tastings, a skilled guide will frequently describe the subtle differences between various types. Take a slow sip, enjoy the flavors, and discuss this highly regarded Oaxacan beverage with others.

Culinary Souvenirs and Keepsakes

Mercado de Artesanías: Culinary Artistry in Handcrafts

Look for mementos with a gastronomic theme at Mercado de Artesanías. You can find distinctive mementos that showcase the region's culinary identity, such as handwoven tablecloths with Oaxacan culinary patterns or elaborately painted molcajetes (stone mortars).

Local Markets: Edible Souvenirs

Buying culinary souvenirs from the local markets will allow you to take a piece of Oaxaca home with you. Keep an eye out for mezcal, mole paste, and handcrafted chocolates; these items capture the essence of Oaxacan flavors. These culinary gems are wonderful keepsakes of your culinary adventure or considerate presents.

Engaging in Culinary Conversations with Locals

Language and Cultural Exchange

Even though most people in tourist destinations speak English, you can improve your culinary experiences by having simple discussions in Spanish. Visitors that make an attempt to speak with locals in their language are greatly appreciated. Acquire some essential culinary expressions, show your gratitude, and create opportunities for meaningful cross-cultural interactions.

Meeting Local Artisans and Chefs

Meet the chefs and artists in your area; they will be happy to talk to you about their work. These interactions deepen your grasp of

Oaxacan culinary traditions, whether it's through studying the intricate details of creating mole or comprehending the craft of traditional pottery.

Final Thoughts: A Culinary Journey Unveiled

In 2024–2025, while you explore Oaxaca's food scene, let every meal serve as a new chapter in your travelogue. Oaxaca's rich food culture invites you to discover, taste, and relish the essence of this wonderful region—from the bustling markets to the tranquil cafes along the shore.

Amidst vivid hues, robust tastes, and the gracious warmth of the Oaxacan people, your gastronomic exploration transforms into a celebration of cultural diversity. Whether you're taking part in cooking classes, going to festivals, or exploring markets, keep in mind that Oaxaca's culinary culture is more than simply food—it's a gateway to the spirit and essence of an alluring place.

Thus, may your senses be stimulated, your taste buds dance with ecstasy, and your memories be seasoned with the unique flavors of Oaxaca as you set off on your culinary adventure. Que disfrutes al maximo y buen provecho! (Good appetite and may you fully enjoy!)

Discovering Oaxaca's Cultural Shades: A Journey through Museums, Historical Sites, and Art Galleries (2024-2025)

Introduction to Oaxaca's Cultural Landscape

As you set off on a cultural tour of Oaxaca in 2024–2025, get ready to be enthralled with the rich legacy, art, and history that make up this fascinating area. Oaxaca provides a rainbow of experiences that mirror the diversity and resiliency of its people, from top-notch museums to intriguing art galleries and historic monuments.

Museums: Gateways to Oaxaca's Past and Present

Oaxacan Cultures Museum, or Museo de las Culturas de Oaxaca

Address: Reforma #704, Centro, 68000 Oaxaca de Juárez, Oax., Mexico **Latitude:** 17.0633° N **Longitude:** 96.7238° W

Housed in the historic Convento de Santo Domingo, the Museo de las Culturas de Oaxaca is a cultural treasure trove. Discover objects representing the indigenous cultures of Oaxaca, from the lively customs of modern villages to the Zapotec and Mixtec civilizations. The merger of pre-Hispanic and colonial elements

46

may be seen in the museum's courtyards and chapels.

Museo Rufino Tamayo

Address: Morelos 503, Ruta Independencia, 68000 Oaxaca de Juárez, Oax., Mexico **Latitude:** 17.0625° N **Longitude:** 96.7247° W

Honoring the popular Oaxacan artist Rufino Tamayo, this museum showcases modern art. Tamayo's masterworks are shown with pieces by other Mexican artists in the collection. The unique combination of paintings, sculptures, and installations is complemented by the museum's contemporary architecture, which creates a vibrant environment for creative inquiry.

Centro Fotográfico Álvarez Bravo

Address: Manuel Bravo 116, Barrio de Jalatlaco, 68080 Oaxaca de Juárez, Oax., Mexico **Latitude:** 17.0651° N **Longitude:** 96.7209° W

Centro Fotográfico Álvarez Bravo is a cultural jewel for photography enthusiasts. The center, named for Manuel Álvarez Bravo, a pioneer in Mexican photography from Oaxaca, features both historical and modern photographic pieces on display. For those interested in Oaxaca's visual storytelling, it's a must-visit because of its compact environment and varied displays.

Historical Sites: Echoes of the Past

Monte Albán Archaeological Site

Address: Carretera al Proyecto Monte Albán, 68000 Oaxaca de Juárez, Oax., Mexico **Latitude:** 17.0430° N **Longitude:** 96.7676° W

Monte Albán, a UNESCO World Heritage Site, is evidence of the highly developed civilizations that had flourished in Oaxaca.

Discover the magnificent pyramids, elaborate sculptures, and ball courts of the former Zapotec capital, all situated against sweeping views of the Oaxacan Valley. Monte Albán transports visitors to the center of Oaxaca during the pre-Hispanic era.

Mitla Archaeological Zone

Address: Av. Ferrocarril, Barrio de San Pablo, 70430 San Pablo Villa de Mitla, Oax., Mexico **Latitude:** 16.9187° N **Longitude:** 96.3659° W

The architectural prowess of the Mixtec and Zapotec cultures is demonstrated by Mitla, another amazing archeological find. Take in the elaborate geometric patterns that cover the walls of Mitla's historic structures, also referred to as the "City of the Dead." The site's unusual blend of ceremonial and religious constructions provides insight into the creators' spiritual convictions.

Art Galleries: Oaxaca's Contemporary Creative Hub

Galería Quetzalli

Address: Macedonio Alcalá 407, Ruta Independencia, 68000 Oaxaca de Juárez, Oax., Mexico **Latitude:** 17.0605° N **Longitude:** 96.7265° W

The vibrant Galería Quetzalli is devoted to modern art. This gallery features both established and up-and-coming artists' work in a variety of exhibitions. Artworks ranging from paintings and sculptures to multimedia projects are showcased at Galería Quetzalli, giving Oaxacan and foreign artists an opportunity to interact with the community.

Instituto de Artes Gráficas de Oaxaca (IAGO)

Address: Macedonio Alcalá 507, Ruta Independencia, 68000

Oaxaca de Juárez, Oax., Mexico **Latitude:** 17.0604° N
Longitude: 96.7267° W

Located in a tastefully renovated colonial building, IAGO serves as
Oaxaca's center for graphic arts. The institute provides a refuge for
people interested in printmaking, graphic design, and the visual
arts, offering exhibitions, courses, and a dedicated library. IAGO's
varied programming demonstrates its dedication to fostering
artistic discourse and cross-cultural exchange.

Cultural Intersection: Markets, Festivals, and Events

Mercado Benito Juarez

Address: Calle Las Casas 712, Col. Reforma, 68050 Oaxaca de
Juárez, Oax., Mexico **Latitude:** 17.0645° N **Longitude:** 96.7281°
W

Mercado Benito Juarez is a great place to experience Oaxaca's
unique cultural weaves outside the typical cultural institutions.
This vibrant market features a display of regional handicrafts,
textiles, and traditional folk art in addition to delicious food.
Explore the winding hallways to find one-of-a-kind items that
capture the essence of Oaxacan ingenuity.

Guelaguetza Festival

Known as "Oaxaca's most beautiful festival," the Guelaguetza
honors the customs and cultures of the indigenous people. Every
year in July, it's a colorful exhibition of dancing, music, and food.
The smells of mole, tamales, and tlayudas fill the marketplaces and
streets, creating a multisensory experience that highlights the
variety of Oaxacan food.

Exploring Oaxaca's Cultural Shades:

Practical Tips

Cultural Etiquette and Respectful Exploration

When visiting Oaxaca's cultural landmarks, show respect for sacred sites and observe local etiquette. Certain archaeological sites may not allow photography, thus it's customary to obtain permission before snapping images. Attending cultural events should be enjoyed while remembering how important it is to uphold customs.

Guided Tours and Cultural Immersion

Take a look at guided tours if you want to learn more about the cultural past of Oaxaca. A well-informed guide may add context and stories to improve your comprehension of historical places, museums, and art galleries. To further engage with the community, take part in cultural immersion activities like seminars and neighborhood gatherings.

Language Considerations

Even though Spanish is widely spoken in tourist regions, knowing a few fundamental words will improve your cross-cultural communication. Making an attempt to speak with locals in their language is greatly appreciated by them as it promotes a closer bond and understanding. To enhance your cultural experience, make use of local language classes or language learning applications.

Conclusion: A Cultural Odyssey Unveiled

In 2024–2025, while you explore Oaxaca's museums, historical monuments, and art galleries, allow each cultural experience to serve as a doorway into the essence of this remarkable place. Stories of resiliency, inventiveness, and the eternal spirit of Oaxaca's people are weaved throughout the city's cultural fabric, which stretches from the historic pyramids of Monte Albán to the modern art galleries of Galería Quetzalli.

I hope that discovering Oaxaca's cultural treasures will leave you feeling amazed, inspired, and deeply appreciative of the many different strands that bind the area's past and present together. May your cultural journey be a life-changing experience that leaves you with enduring memories and a greater understanding of this cultural oasis as you stand in the shadow of ancient civilizations, marvel at modern artistic manifestations, and interact with the live traditions of Oaxaca. Cheers to Oaxaca! (May Oaxaca live long!)

Off the Beaten Path: Hidden Cultural Gems

Textile Museum of Oaxaca (Museo Textil de Oaxaca)

Address: Hidalgo 917, Centro, 68000 Oaxaca de Juárez, Oax., Mexico **Latitude:** 17.0652° N **Longitude:** 96.7206° W

Embracing the creativity of traditional textiles, the Textile Museum is a hidden gem located in the core of Oaxaca's historic district. Discover an enchanting array of woven textiles, clothing, and weaves that highlight the elaborate methods and vivid hues that characterize Oaxacan textile customs. The museum provides an insight into the importance of textiles to the local culture.

Ethnobotanical Garden of Oaxaca (Jardín Etnobotánico de Oaxaca)

Address: Reforma 602, Ruta Independencia, 68000 Oaxaca de Juárez, Oax., Mexico **Latitude:** 17.0605° N **Longitude:** 96.7224° W

Enter the Ethnobotanical Garden, a place where nature and culture collide. This living museum highlights the plants utilized in traditional medicine, rituals, and handcrafted products, showcasing

Oaxaca's rich botanical diversity. Explore the verdant gardens while being escorted by the ancient indigenous knowledge that dates back centuries and learn about the profound relationship that exists between Oaxaca's rich floral heritage and its culture.

Oaxacan Arts and Crafts: Markets beyond Benito Juarez

Mercado de Artesanías de la Plaza Labastida

Address: Calle de Mina, Centro, 68000 Oaxaca de Juárez, Oax., Mexico **Latitude:** 17.0658° N **Longitude:** 96.7253° W

Visit Mercado de Artesanías de la Plaza Labastida for a more intimate, locally owned shopping experience, even if Mercado Benito Juarez is a center for crafts. Artists display their handcrafted items here, such as textiles, ceramics, and colorful folk art sculptures called alebrijes. Interact with the craftspeople, see how they come up with their designs, and bring home one-of-a-kind items that showcase the variety of Oaxacan artistry.

Tianguis Cultural de Oaxaca

Address: Calle Miguel Hidalgo, Colonia Reforma, 68050 Oaxaca de Juárez, Oax., Mexico **Latitude:** 17.0598° N **Longitude:** 96.7268° W

Every week, Oaxaca's Tianguis Cultural de Oaxaca turns the streets into a bustling exhibition of the region's handicrafts and artwork. Local craftspeople erect booths here, selling anything from traditional clothes to handcrafted jewelry. The tianguis offers an engaging environment for direct interaction with artists, allowing one to learn about their sources of inspiration.

Cultural Fusion: Music, Dance, and Traditional Performances

Casa de la Cultura de Oaxaca (House of Culture)

Address: Avenida Juarez 203, Ruta Independencia, 68000 Oaxaca de Juárez, Oax., Mexico **Latitude:** 17.0632° N **Longitude:** 96.7253° W

The center of Oaxacan artistic and cultural activity is the Casa de la Cultura. See theatrical shows, music recitals, and traditional dance performances that highlight the rich cultural legacy of the area. See what's happening this weekend at the cultural center and get lost in the rhythms and movements that characterize Oaxaca's performing arts scene.

Zócalo: A Stage for Cultural Celebrations

Oaxaca's main square, the Zócalo, serves as both a hub for social gatherings and a platform for impromptu cultural events. The Zócalo comes alive with Oaxacan culture, from spontaneous musical performances to dance troupes demonstrating traditional choreography. If you take a leisurely stroll around the square, you can come across local artists displaying their artistic expressions in different formats.

Sustainable Tourism and Cultural Preservation

Supporting Local Artisans and Communities

Encourage ethical tourism by giving back to the communities and craftspeople in your area. When buying crafts or going to cultural events, give priority to companies and projects that improve the quality of life for the local populace. By your support, ancient crafts are preserved and will be available to future generations.

Eco-friendly Cultural Experiences

Investigate sustainable cultural activities that are friendly to the environment. Take into account workshops and guided tours that place an emphasis on protecting the environment and honoring cultural heritage. Making environmentally friendly decisions helps to protect Oaxaca's scenic landscape and rich cultural heritage.

The Ongoing Cultural Story: Oaxaca's Living Heritage

As you proceed with your cultural discovery of Oaxaca, keep in mind that the real spirit of this place is found in the living legacy of its people, not merely in its historical relics and works of art. You become a part of Oaxaca's continuous cultural narrative whether you're taking in the vivid ambiance of the local markets, touring ancient ruins, or interacting with modern artists.

Every step you take through historical buildings, museums, and art galleries is an invitation to enter Oaxaca's heart, where customs are passed down through the ages, creativity is unrestricted, and the past and present coexist peacefully. I hope that your time spent experiencing Oaxaca culture will be a celebration of variety, a means of bridging cultures, and an example of the resilient spirit of a place that keeps adding its own narrative to the annals of human history. Cheers to Oaxaca's culture! (Long live Oaxacan culture!)

Navigating Oaxaca's Cultural Calendar

Festival de la Ciudad de Oaxaca

Attend the Festival de la Ciudad to feel Oaxaca's pulse. This yearly festival features a wide range of cultural events, such as music concerts, traditional dances, and parades. The city bursts into a riot of color, noise, and joyous celebration. Make sure your visit coincides with this exciting cultural spectacle by consulting the festival schedule.

Noche de Rabanos (Night of the Radishes)

A distinctive Oaxacan custom known as Noche de Rabanos is observed on December 23rd. Radishes are transformed into beautiful pieces of art by artisans who carve detailed scenes and figures out of them. Take a leisurely stroll through Oaxaca on this joyous evening, admire the sculptures made of radish, and observe the artistic expression that abounds during this yearly occasion.

Cultural Insights: Engaging with Local Communities

Community-based Tourism Initiatives

Engage in tourist projects that are grounded in the community and offer genuine opportunities for connection with locals. Visits to native communities, where you can partake in customary crafts, farming methods, and cultural ceremonies, are frequently part of these programs. You can support sustainable tourism and learn more about Oaxacan culture by becoming fully immersed in the daily lives of the locals.

Homestays and Cultural Exchanges

For a more comprehensive cultural encounter, think about homestays. You can witness everyday routines, share meals, and have meaningful conversations when you live with a local family. Through the removal of barriers and the development of enduring relationships, homestays promote cross-cultural interactions between tourists and Oaxacan people.

Oaxaca's Cultural Resilience: Post-Pandemic Reflections

Artistic Responses to Adversity

See the ways that Oaxacan cultural organizations and artists addressed the issues brought up by the worldwide health crisis.

Many of them made the transition to online platforms, including digital performances, virtual tours, and online exhibitions. Examine the ways in which the artistic community overcame hardship to show the resiliency of Oaxaca's cultural landscape.

Sustainable Tourism Practices in the Post-Pandemic Era

Sustainable tourism techniques have become increasingly important since the pandemic. Examine Oaxaca's adoption of eco-friendly programs, locally driven tourism, and responsible travel choices. Interact with companies and groups that put the welfare of tourists and the neighborhood's environment first.

Future Directions: Preserving and Innovating Culture

Cultural Preservation Efforts

Find out what is being done to maintain Oaxaca's cultural legacy. From conservation projects at archaeological sites to programs aimed at preserving traditional crafts, find out about the joint efforts that are being made to ensure that the essence of Oaxacan culture is preserved for future generations.

Innovation in Cultural Expression

Discover how Oaxaca's creative expressions are influencing the city's ongoing cultural evolution. See the vibrant innovation that characterizes Oaxaca's 21st-century cultural landscape, from modern art installations to fusion performances that combine traditional and modern elements.

Reflections on Your Cultural Journey

As your cultural journey across Oaxaca comes to an end, pause to consider the variety of experiences, deep connections, and fresh insights you have acquired. The cultural fabric of Oaxaca is dynamic and ever-evolving, shaped by the interaction of tradition and innovation, resiliency and adaptability.

Whether you have engaged with local artists, danced to traditional music, or marveled at ancient pyramids, your experience has become a part of the ongoing story of Oaxaca's cultural legacy. Take with you the memories of colorful markets, enthralling shows, and the friendly friendliness that characterizes Oaxacan culture as you bid adieu to this amazing place.

Think about how your interactions and experiences have helped to preserve and celebrate Oaxaca's cultural legacy as you reflect on your experiences. Spread awareness of the depth and variety that characterize Oaxacan culture throughout the world by sharing your experiences, photos, and thoughts with others.

Conclusion: A Cultural Shade Unveiled

You've set out on an extraordinary voyage as you explore the museums, historical sites, markets, and cultural events of Oaxaca in 2024–2025. The cultural weaves of Oaxaca is a live representation of the people who have shaped it over generations, not just a collection of objects and performances.

I hope that your cultural research in Oaxaca will inspire you and help people realize how intertwined all civilizations are and how beautiful it can be when different customs come together. May the vibrant cultural weaves of Oaxaca continue to enthrall and unfold as you carry it with you, bridging boundaries and building understanding between the world's weaves. Farewell, Oaxaca! (Until our next encounter, Oaxaca!)

Exploring Oaxaca's Natural Wonders: A Journey into the Heart of Breathtaking Landscapes (2024-2025)

Introduction to Oaxaca's Natural Beauty

Get ready to be fascinated by the many and breathtaking natural treasures that make up this fascinating region as you travel through Oaxaca. The landscapes of Oaxaca offer a symphony of beauty and biodiversity, from the mineral-rich lakes of Hierve el Agua to the sun-kissed beaches along the Oaxacan Coast and the ancient archaeological wonders of Monte Albán and Mitla.

Hierve el Agua: The Petrified Waterfalls

Location and Accessibility

Address: Hierve el Agua, San Lorenzo Albarradas, Oax., Mexico
Latitude: 17.2858° N **Longitude:** 97.1481° W

Tucked away in the mountains of Oaxaca, Hierve el Agua is a stunning natural formation that seems to be made of stone formed by water. The drive to Hierve el Agua passes through picturesque scenery that reveals hints of Oaxaca's rustic charm. The location is reachable by car and is about 70 kilometers east of Oaxaca City.

Petrified Cascades and Natural Pools

"Boiling water" in Spanish, Hierve el Agua is known for its pools full of minerals and petrified waterfalls. The tumbling cliffs provide the impression of frozen waterfalls, as colorful, terraced structures are left behind by mineral-rich springs. Aside from swimming in the natural pools and admiring the breathtaking views of the neighboring valleys and mountains, visitors can wonder at the cascades.

Cultural Significance and Local Flora

In addition to its natural wonders, Hierve el Agua is important to the native Zapotec communities culturally. The surrounding flora, which includes agave plants, enhances the scenic environment, and the place is thought to have therapeutic benefits. Talk to local guides to learn more about Hierve el Agua's ecological and cultural value.

Monte Albán: Ancient City in the Clouds

Location and Historical Significance

Address: Carretera A Monte Albán Km. 6, 71230 Santa Cruz Xoxocotlán, Oax., Mexico **Latitude:** 17.0430° N **Longitude:** 96.7676° W

Monte Albán, on a mountain plateau, is a reminder of the Zapotecs' highly developed civilization. Declared a UNESCO World Heritage Site, the archeological site provides an enthralling tour of pre-Hispanic Oaxaca. Accessible for day visits or longer investigation, Monte Albán is only a short drive from Oaxaca City.

Ancient Pyramids and Temples

Discover the Zapotec people's mastery of architecture and art with a visit to the expansive Monte Albán complex, which is home to majestic pyramids, ceremonial platforms, and finely carved stelae. Three significant buildings that take tourists back in time are the Main Plaza, the Observatory, and the Ball Court. Discover the wonders of this ancient city in the skies by interacting with informed advisors.

Panoramic Views of Oaxaca Valley

The magnificent sweeping vistas of the Oaxaca Valley that Monte Albán offers are among its main attractions. Admire the majesty of the surrounding mountains and the meeting place of nature and prehistoric civilization from high vantage points. Monte Albán's advantageous location offers a visual feast that highlights its importance as a hub for culture and ceremonies.

Mitla: The City of the Dead

Location and Architectural Marvels

Address: Av. Ferrocarril, Barrio de San Pablo, 70430 San Pablo Villa de Mitla, Oax., Mexico **Latitude:** 16.9187° N **Longitude:** 96.3659° W

Oaxaca's Mitla is another archaeological treasure that is known for its distinctive architectural design and elaborate geometric patterns. The location is roughly 46 kilometers east of Oaxaca City in the Valley of Tlacolula. History and architecture buffs can not miss Mitla because of its uniquely decorated buildings and UNESCO World Heritage Site designation.

Intricate Mosaic and Zapotec Symbolism

In contrast to other archeological sites, Mitla is distinguished by its fine stone sculptures and mosaic fretwork. The tiny stone fragments that make up the geometric patterns, called grecas, are carefully placed together. In addition to demonstrating the Zapotecs' exceptional mechanical prowess, these patterns have symbolic meaning in Zapotec theology and mythology.

Courtyards, Tombs, and the Columns of Mitla

Stroll around Mitla's courtyards and you'll come upon the Columns Group, a group of columns with ornate carvings on them. The skill of the Zapotec craftspeople is demonstrated by these columns. Investigate the underground passageways and tombs to learn more about Mitla's significance as a spiritual hub and a place of sacred entombment.

The Oaxacan Coast: Sun-Kissed Serenity

Puerto Escondido: Surfing Haven

Address: Puerto Escondido, Oax., Mexico **Latitude:** 15.8497° N **Longitude:** 97.0657° W

Go to the sunny beaches of Puerto Escondido on the coast of Oaxacan and unwind. This seaside resort, known for its world-class surfing conditions, welcomes both beachgoers and aquatic aficionados. Relaxation and adventure are well combined at Puerto Escondido, with its golden beaches, lively markets, and laid-back vibe.

Mazunte: Turtle Sanctuary and Beach Bliss

Address: Mazunte, Oax., Mexico **Latitude:** 15.6675° N **Longitude:** 96.5507° W

Explore the tranquil community of Mazunte, famous for its immaculate beaches and dedication to preservation of the environment. The National Mexican Turtle Center is located near Mazunte, where visitors may observe the release of newborn turtles into the ocean and learn about efforts to conserve the marine environment. For those in search of peace and stunning scenery, Mazunte's serene beaches offer a refuge.

Zipolite: Clothing-Optional Paradise

Address: Zipolite, Oax., Mexico **Latitude:** 15.6561° N **Longitude:** 96.5018° W

One of the few beaches in Mexico where clothes is not required,

Zipolite calls to visitors looking for a freeing experience. Accept the laid-back vibe of this beachside community, where the sound of the Pacific waves combines with the carefree attitudes of the visitors. Attracting visitors from all over the world, Zipolite is a cultural melting pot as well as a beach resort.

Exploring Oaxaca's Natural Wonders: Practical Tips

Sustainable Tourism and Conservation

While taking in the natural beauty of Oaxaca, consider supporting sustainable tourism practices. Observe conservation rules, especially in protected regions, and show respect for the native ecosystems by staying on approved pathways. Take part in environmentally conscious programs that help to protect Oaxaca's scenic surroundings.

Guided Tours and Interpretive Programs

To further deepen your understanding of Oaxaca's natural beauties, think about participating in guided tours and informative programs. At locations like Hierve el Agua, Monte Albán, Mitla, and the Oaxacan Coast, knowledgeable guides offer insights on the geological, historical, and cultural aspects of the area. Your relationship with the landscapes and their significance is strengthened by these encounters.

Responsible Beach Practices

As you visit the Oaxacan Coast, remember to be mindful of proper beach behavior. Honor wildlife, refrain from polluting, and keep in mind the fragile ecosystems that exist along the coast. Select marine activity providers who uphold ethical standards to guarantee the long-term viability of Oaxaca's coastal ecosystems.

Conclusion: Nature's Symphony in

Oaxaca

In Oaxaca, the landscapes become more than just geological formations; they are chapters in the Earth's narrative that reveal the intricate dance of time, culture, and natural forces. You can experience this symphony of nature as you walk through the mineral-laden pools of Hierve el Agua, stand atop the ancient pyramids of Monte Albán, explore the mosaic wonders of Mitla, and feel the gentle embrace of the Oaxacan Coast.

I hope your tour of Oaxaca's natural treasures is a melodic one, with each location revealing a distinct tune that combines the ageless beat of the Pacific waves, the spirit of the Zapotec people, and the echoes of bygone eras. You become a witness to the poetry that nature herself has written in this unique part of the globe when you take in the splendor of Hierve el Agua, the history of Monte Albán, the artistry of Mitla, and the tranquility of the Oaxacan Coast. ¡Viva Oaxaca's natural beauty! (Long live Oaxaca's natural beauty!)

Hierve el Agua: A Geological Masterpiece Unveiled

Ecological Diversity and Flora

In addition to being a geological marvel, Hierve el Agua is a hotspot for biological richness. Numerous plant species, including endemic ones that have adapted to the special mineral-rich environment, beautify the surrounding area. Understanding the site's biological subtleties improves one's understanding of the precarious equilibrium between biology and geology.

Hiking Trails and Ecotourism

Embrace the opportunity to see Hierve el Agua's natural beauty by exploring the well-kept paths that wind across the area. Along with providing amazing views of the petrified waterfalls, these pathways provide an opportunity to see native plants and animals. Birdwatching and nature hikes are two ecotourism activities that help you get in touch with Oaxaca's natural heritage.

Sustainable Practices and Community Involvement

Initiatives aimed at promoting sustainable tourism now center around Hierve el Agua. By taking action to reduce their negative effects on the environment, local communities actively contribute to maintaining the area's ecological integrity. Visitors can ensure that Hierve el Agua is preserved as a pure natural treasure for future generations by supporting projects led by the local community and selecting ethical tour operators.

Monte Albán: Unraveling the Mysteries of an Ancient City

Ongoing Archaeological Discoveries

Excavations at Monte Albán are still being conducted, and they are uncovering new facets of the city's past. The unearthing of graves, relics, and elaborate carvings offers new perspectives on the daily routine, spiritual rituals, and cultural development of the Zapotec people. As archaeologists reveal the mysteries hidden beneath the historic city, visitors may observe the meeting point of the past and modern.

Night Tours and Astronomical Significance

You should think about taking one of Monte Albán's night tours for a memorable experience. The historic pyramids and buildings in the Oaxaca Valley take on an otherworldly appearance when the sun sets. Tour guides narrate tales of the heavenly importance ingrained in the design of the city, emphasizing the Zapotec people's profound cosmic connection. From this archaeological site, stargazing offers a reflective voyage through time.

Educational Programs and Cultural Exchange

Monte Albán functions as a center for education, providing tourists with interactive programming. Through interactive demonstrations, educational workshops, and cultural exchange programs, one can gain a deeper understanding of Zapotec culture and the archeological techniques used to solve the secrets of Monte Albán. These events encourage tourists to interact actively with Oaxaca's living history.

Mitla: Artistry Carved in Stone

Preservation Efforts and Restoration Projects

Continuous preservation efforts are needed for Mitla's elaborate stone carvings and distinctive architectural elements. The preservation of Mitla's structural integrity is the major goal of restoration initiatives overseen by specialists in archaeology and cultural heritage. Viewers can observe these preservation efforts and learn about the painstaking methods used to protect the place for future generations.

Indigenous Artisans and Craftsmanship

Interact with native craftspeople in the area who have carried on Mitla's long-standing craft traditions. These craftspeople frequently replicate Mitla's elaborate designs, demonstrating the persistence of artistic methods that have their roots in Zapotec culture. Buying locally created goods helps preserve Mitla's cultural heritage in addition to benefiting the neighborhood.

Nighttime Illumination and Cultural Performances

See Mitla from a new perspective, literally. The archaeological site becomes a captivating scene when illuminated at night. Mitla's architectural elements and spiritual significance can be appreciated by visitors in a wonderful atmosphere created by special activities and cultural performances staged during these illuminated nights.

The Oaxacan Coast: Sun, Sand, and Sustainable Tourism

Ecotourism Initiatives and Marine Conservation

With its immaculate beaches and abundant marine life, the Oaxacan Coast has emerged as a key destination for ecotourism projects. Local people take an active role in marine conservation initiatives, safeguarding sea turtle breeding grounds and maintaining the delicate balance of coastal ecosystems. By participating in ecotourism activities like beach clean-ups and guided snorkeling tours, visitors can help ensure the Oaxacan Coast remains sustainable.

Responsible Whale Watching and Bird watching

Along the Oaxacan Coast, there are certain places to go whale watching that promote safe behavior. Travelers can experience the breathtaking spectacle of migratory whales, such as gray and humpback whales, during certain seasons. Lagoons and estuaries along the coast are home to a variety of bird species that are worth exploring for birdwatchers. Minimal disruption to these natural ecosystems is ensured by responsible wildlife observing procedures.

Community-Run Beach Conservation Programs

Community-run beach conservation programs have been formed in a number of coastal towns. These programs are aimed at monitoring marine biodiversity, safeguarding sea turtle nests, and encouraging appropriate beach behavior. By actively engaging in these activities, visitors can get a firsthand understanding of the difficulties and successes faced in protecting the natural gems of the Oaxacan Coast.

Beyond Boundaries: Connecting with Oaxaca's Natural Heritage

Cross-Cultural Collaboration in Conservation

The natural treasures of Oaxaca act as links between many cultural contexts, encouraging intercultural cooperation in conservation efforts. Local communities work with international researchers, environmentalists, and conservationists to adopt sustainable practices. Knowledge and skill sharing makes ensuring that conservation initiatives respect Oaxaca's traditional values as well as scientific concepts.

Nature-Based Cultural Experiences

Discovering Oaxaca's natural treasures in a comprehensive way is possible through nature-based cultural experiences. Visitors can engage with the spiritual and cultural aspects of Oaxaca's natural heritage through yoga retreats, meditation sessions, and wellness programs held in the middle of natural surroundings. These encounters encourage a balanced coexistence between environmental conservation and cultural appreciation.

Storytelling and Indigenous Wisdom

Accept the role that storytelling plays in conserving ecological knowledge and indigenous wisdom. Stories of past civilizations, geological formations, and the complex interrelationship between humans and nature are told by local guides and community members. The natural and cultural history of Oaxaca is woven together richly by these stories.

Sustainable Travel Tips for Exploring Oaxaca's Natural Wonders

Respect for Indigenous Communities

Respect the indigenous groups whose traditions are entwined with the breathtaking natural features of Oaxaca. Ask permission before visiting places of worship, interact with local guides, and back community-led projects that put sustainable tourism and cultural preservation first.

Minimize Ecological Footprint

Reduce your environmental impact by adhering to the Leave No Trace philosophy. Refrain from littering, stay on trails that are designated, and follow any environmental advice that tour companies and conservation groups may provide. The ecosystems of Oaxaca will be preserved for future generations if responsible behavior is practiced.

Support Local Conservation Initiatives

Support neighborhood projects and groups devoted to protecting the area's natural and cultural heritage to help with Oaxaca's ongoing conservation efforts. Travelers are essential to maintaining the beauty of Oaxaca's landscapes, whether by donations, volunteer work, or involvement in community-led initiatives.

Reflections on Nature's Shade: A Journey of Harmony

Take a minute to contemplate as you finish exploring the mineral-rich waters of Hierve el Agua, look up at the historic pyramids of Monte Albán, are in awe of the artistic carvings of Mitla, and feel the smooth sands of the Oaxacan Coast beneath your feet. You have traveled across temporal, cultural, and biological landscapes in addition to actual ones.

Oaxaca is a place where nature's weaves is displayed via the colors of stunning geological formations, fascinating archeological sites, and the radiant sunlight of coastal vistas. Every location has a narrative to tell that cuts over national boundaries, connects with the knowledge of indigenous people, and challenges you to take up the role of keeper of Oaxaca's natural and cultural heritage.

Epilogue: A Symphony of Gratitude

As you bid adieu to Oaxaca's natural beauties, be thankful that you have the opportunity to experience a symphony that the Earth has created. The sun-kissed beaches, ancient pyramids, petrified waterfalls, and mosaic-adorned buildings have all shared their tunes with you. May these harmonies encourage you to dedicate your life to protecting and honoring the magnificent weaves of Oaxaca's natural heritage as you carry them in your heart. Thank you, Oaxaca! (Grateful, Oaxaca!)

Setting out on Outdoor Adventures in Oaxaca: A Comprehensive Guide (2024-2025)

Introduction to Oaxaca's Outdoor Playground

Outdoor lovers are drawn to Oaxaca by its varied landscapes, which include sun-kissed beaches and hilly mountains. The key to exploring the vast array of outdoor activities Oaxaca has to offer in 2024–2025 is this guide. Oaxaca's outdoor playground offers activities for all types of visitors, including those who enjoy trekking, beaching, and ecotourism.

Hiking and Trekking: Ascending Oaxaca's Peaks

Sierra Norte: Trails through Cloud Forests

Address: Sierra Norte, Oaxaca, Mexico **Latitude:** 17.2631° N **Longitude:** 96.6436° W

This area, which is tucked away in the Sierra Norte mountain range, has a network of paths that run through cloud forests and provide sweeping views over the valleys of Oaxaca. Trek through places such as Llano Grande, Benito Juarez, and others to get a sense of the Zapotec people's diverse cultural heritage. Trails range in difficulty to accommodate hikers of all skill levels.

Hierve el Agua to Roaring Waterfalls

Address: Hierve el Agua, San Lorenzo Albarradas, Oaxaca, Mexico **Latitude:** 17.2858° N **Longitude:** 97.1481° W

Set out on a picturesque hike from Hierve el Agua's petrified waterfalls to the neighboring thunderous waterfalls. Before you reach the gushing waterfalls, the walk passes through untamed scenery where you may observe Hierve el Agua's natural treasures. This hike offers an unforgettable outdoor experience by fusing scenic natural beauty with strenuous physical terrain.

Cerro San Felipe: Summit with a View

Address: Cerro San Felipe, Oaxaca, Mexico **Latitude:** 17.0983° N **Longitude:** 96.6923° W

A strenuous trek to Cerro San Felipe culminates in magnificent views of Oaxaca City and the surrounding lowlands. The trail passes through a variety of environments, including rocky outcrops and oak woodlands. See vistas of native plants and animals as you ascend. A rewarding trekker's reward for reaching the peak is a panoramic spectacle, which makes it a must-visit.

Beach Activities: Sun, Surf, and Serenity

Puerto Escondido: Surfer's Paradise

Address: Puerto Escondido, Oaxaca, Mexico **Latitude:** 15.8497° N **Longitude:** 97.0657° W

With its strong waves, Puerto Escondido is a surfer's dream come true. The beaches of Puerto Escondido provide a variety of surf breaks suitable for all skill levels, regardless of experience level. Take surfing lessons, hire a board, and hit the waves at Playa Zicatela, one of the top surf spots in the world.

Zipolite: Beach Bliss and Naturism

Address: Zipolite, Oaxaca, Mexico **Latitude:** 15.6561° N

Longitude: 96.5018° W

Known for its casual vibe, Zipolite is one of the few beaches in Mexico where clothes are not required. The golden sands and Pacific waves of Zipolite make for the perfect beach experience, whether you're a naturist or just looking for a laid-back beach day. Enjoy fresh seafood from coastal restaurants, do beach yoga, and take in the tranquility of the setting sun.

Mazunte: Turtle Conservation and Tranquil Beaches

Address: Mazunte, Oaxaca, Mexico **Latitude:** 15.6675° N **Longitude:** 96.5507° W

In addition to having immaculate beaches, Mazunte is a center for the preservation of sea turtles. Take part in the releasing of newborn turtles under supervision as they make their way to the ocean. Mazunte's beaches, such Playa Rinconcito, offer a peaceful environment for swimming, sunbathing, and soaking up the allure of the coast.

Ecotourism Options: Connecting with Nature Responsibly

Laguna de Manialtepec: Bioluminescent Magic

Address: Laguna de Manialtepec, Oaxaca, Mexico **Latitude:** 15.9581° N **Longitude:** 97.2365° W

Set out on an enthralling ecotourism journey in Laguna de Manialtepec, recognized for its waters that glow with light. Take a guided night trip to experience the wonders of bioluminescence, where the movement of marine bacteria creates a shimmering effect in the water. You may minimize your ecological effect while marveling at the marvels of nature with this eco-friendly experience.

Copalita Eco-Archaeological Park: Nature and History

Address: Copalita Eco-Archaeological Park, Huatulco, Oaxaca, Mexico **Latitude:** 15.7273° N **Longitude:** 96.2494° W

Discover the Copalita Eco-Archaeological Park, a place where history and nature meet. Archaeological ruins surrounded by lush greenery and a variety of bird species can be found at this ecotourism site. Explore the park's winding pathways, which provide views of the fauna that flourishes in this protected area as well as historical civilizations.

Oaxacan Orchid Reserves: Botanical Beauty

Address: Various Orchid Reserves, Oaxaca, Mexico **Latitude:** Varies by Reserve **Longitude:** Varies by Reserve

Visit an orchid refuge in Oaxaca to learn about its botanical splendor. Many orchid species, some of which are native to the region, can be found in Oaxaca. Explore these areas, take in the brilliant hues of the orchids in bloom, and discover the significance of orchid conservation for Oaxaca's ecosystems by joining a guided orchid tour.

Exploring Oaxaca's Outdoor Adventures: Practical Tips

Sustainable Hiking Practices

Hiking sustainably is advised in Oaxaca's hilly areas. To prevent upsetting the surrounding ecosystems, stay on authorized trails, bring reusable water bottles, and dispose of all rubbish. Interact with local guides who place an emphasis on safe trekking practices and environmental conservation.

Surfing Etiquette and Safety

Learn about surfing safety precautions and etiquette if you intend to surf at Puerto Escondido. Remember to be considerate of other surfers, be aware of your ability level in relation to the wave conditions, and show respect to the local surf community. Beginners should think about getting surf lessons because safety is of the utmost importance.

Responsible Beach Activities

Engage in ethical beach activities, whether you're lounging on Zipolite's clothing-optional beach or helping to release turtles in Mazunte. To guarantee the preservation of Oaxaca's coastal habitats, refrain from leaving behind trash, show consideration for wildlife, and abide by any municipal ordinances.

Eco-Friendly Tours and Operators

Select eco-friendly tours and operators that place a high priority on sustainability and conservation when partaking in ecotourism activities. Look into tour operators who have won praise for their dedication to reducing their negative effects on the environment and encouraging environmentally conscious travel.

Conclusion: A Symphony of Nature's Adventures

As you get to the end of your outdoor journey in Oaxaca, consider the adventures you have had in the symphony of nature. Oaxaca has shown its many melodies, from the mountain paths of Sierra Norte to the surfer's paradise of Puerto Escondido and the bioluminescent magic of Laguna de Manialtepec.

Remember that your outdoor experiences in Oaxaca are more than simply one-time events as you cherish the memories of strolling through cloud forests, riding waves, and relaxing on immaculate beaches. They are woven together within the rich fabric of Oaxaca's natural history. Every footfall, every wave, every silent moment of reflection adds to the harmony of Oaxaca's outdoor symphony.

In keeping with the idea of sustainable exploration, let your travels cultivate a profound respect for Oaxaca's natural beauties. May the peace of Oaxaca's landscapes be reflected in your times of calm, your waves of delight blend with the rhythm of the Pacific, and your footsteps resound with respect for indigenous customs. ¡Viva la aventura en Oaxaca al free aire! (Long live Oaxaca's outdoor adventures!)

Beyond the Horizon: Extended Outdoor Expeditions

Multi-Day Hiking Trails in Sierra Norte

Sierra Norte offers multi-day hiking trails that wind through isolated communities, cloud forests, and alpine scenery for intrepid hikers looking for a longer journey. Take into consideration hiking the "Pueblos Mancomunados" path, a system of trails maintained by the community that links a number of communities. With this all-encompassing adventure, you may venture deep into the Sierra Norte, enjoying authentic Zapotec food, engaging with people, and camping in primitive cabins.

Coastal Trekking: Puerto Escondido to Zipolite

Set off on a hike along the coast that links the relaxed beaches of Zipolite with the energetic surf town of Puerto Escondido. Trekking along the Pacific coastline over many days offers breathtaking views of the ocean, access to secluded coves, and opportunities to see a variety of marine life. Make lodging arrangements in coastal communities along the route to fully experience each beach community's distinct ambience.

Nature Retreats in Oaxacan Orchid Reserves

Consider participating in nature retreats run in Oaxacan orchid reserves if you're attracted by the botanical wonders of Oaxaca. These multi-day getaways offer guided treks through the reserves, in-depth analyses of several orchid species, and insights into conservation initiatives pertaining to orchids. Experience the world of orchids while taking in the peace and quiet of Oaxaca's natural surroundings.

Adapting to the Rhythms: Outdoor Yoga and Meditation

Mountain Retreats in Sierra Norte

Take advantage of outdoor yoga and meditation retreats to detach from the stresses of everyday life and appreciate the tranquility of Oaxaca's highlands. With its serene surroundings, Sierra Norte offers the perfect environment for reviving your body and mind and fostering a connection with nature. Participate in planned retreats that offer a comprehensive experience by fusing meditation, outdoor yoga classes, and cultural immersions.

Beachside Yoga in Zipolite and Mazunte

On the sandy beaches of Zipolite and Mazunte, practice yoga and take in the soothing effects of the Pacific Ocean. A lot of yoga schools and retreat facilities along the beach provide courses that utilize the healing sounds of the waves and the soft ocean breeze. Take advantage of the natural beauty of Oaxaca's coastal scenery while improving your yoga practice by attending a sunrise or sunset class.

Copalita Eco-Archaeological Park: Meditative Walks

Experience mindfulness in the great outdoors by taking contemplative strolls around Copalita Eco-Archaeological Park's tranquil settings. Walking meditations are a great way to connect with the energy of the surrounding lush foliage, historic ruins, and bird-filled skies. You can appreciate the merging of history, nature, and inner serenity through this meditation experience.

Practical Considerations for Extended Outdoor Pursuits

Wilderness Safety and Preparedness

Prioritize wilderness safety and readiness before setting out on multi-day excursions or lengthy outdoor adventures. Make sure you have enough food, water, emergency supplies, and navigational aids. Learn about the area wildlife, flora, and weather, as well as trail rules. When going on walks near the seashore, keep an eye out for potential dangers and tide schedules.

Responsible Camping Practices

If you plan to camp, make sure you camp responsibly to reduce your influence on the environment. When available, select permitted camping places, abide by the Leave No Trace philosophy, and obey fire safety regulations. Be mindful of the ecosystems you come across and leave them untouched so that future generations can enjoy them.

Cultural Sensitivity in Indigenous Communities

Prioritize cultural awareness when interacting with indigenous tribes on long-term outdoor trips. Ask permission before entering villages, observe local traditions with grace, and take into account the cultural significance of the areas you travel through. Discover the customs of the communities you come across and cultivate constructive relationships that advance understanding between cultures.

Conclusion: Prolonged Harmony with Oaxaca's Outdoors

You become a part of the long-term harmony of Oaxaca's outdoors as you expand your outdoor experiences there, going from day hikes to multi-day expeditions and including mindfulness techniques into your travels. Whether they are coastal or alpine, the landscapes act as a canvas and a backdrop for your experiences, enabling you to establish a closer bond with the natural world.

Beyond the horizon is a vast playground where the natural rhythms of Oaxaca transform into a continuous heartbeat that is in tune with the Pacific's thundering waves, the Sierra Norte's pulse, and the contemplative murmurs of long-gone archaeological sites. Every stride, every stretch, every quiet moment adds to the long-term harmony with Oaxaca's natural treasures.

I hope that your lengthy outdoor adventures in Oaxaca will be a voyage of self-awareness, cultural learning, and environmental conservation. I hope that the sounds of Oaxaca's outdoor spaces will never cease to evoke wonder, thankfulness, and a deep sense of connection to the natural world around you as you explore its many landscapes and partake in long outdoor pursuits. ¡Viva la armonía en Oaxaca al aire libre! (Long live the peace in Oaxaca's countryside!)

Discovering Oaxaca's Markets and Shopping Delights (2024-2025)

Introduction: The Heartbeat of Oaxacan Commerce

Take a sensory tour of Oaxaca's bustling marketplaces and retail areas, where the sound of business transactions complements the rich cultural mosaic of this treasure of Mexico. This in-depth journey takes us on an exploration of the vibrant Mercado Benito Juarez, delves into the realm of arts and crafts, and reveals the hidden gems of regional mementos. Explore the streets, take in the hues, and lose yourself in the distinctive retail experiences Oaxaca has to offer.

Mercado Benito Juarez: A Culinary and Cultural Oasis

Address and Location

Address: Mercado Benito Juarez, Calle de Las Casas, Centro, Oaxaca, Mexico **Latitude:** 17.0653° N **Longitude:** 96.7266° W

Mercado Benito Juarez, a busy marketplace that captures the spirit of Oaxacan cuisine and culture, is located in the Centro of Oaxaca. The market, which has the name of the popular Mexican president Benito Juarez, is a maze-like collection of stands that sell a wide range of goods, from traditional handicrafts to fresh vegetables and spices.

Culinary Exploration: Flavors of Oaxaca

A food lover's paradise, Mercado Benito Juarez has an enticing selection of Oaxacan specialties. Explore the world of mole, a staple of Oaxacan cuisine known for its rich and nuanced sauce. Try the tlayudas, a staple of the area that resembles a big, thin tortilla topped with a variety of toppings. The food area of the market is a symphony of flavors, colors, and fragrances, making it the perfect place to explore different cuisines.

Traditional Handicrafts: A Shopping Extravaganza

You will come across kiosks with colorful textiles, intricately crafted ceramics, and traditional Oaxacan apparel as you make your way through the market's winding hallways. Real-time demonstrations of artisans' abilities offer a singular chance to see the production of handcrafted masterpieces. Strike a deal with neighborhood sellers, and use the market to serve as your entryway to genuine Oaxacan workmanship.

Arts and Crafts: Unveiling Oaxaca's Artistic Heritage

Oaxacan Alebrijes: Whimsical Woodcrafts

Location: Various Artisan Studios, Oaxaca, Mexico

Explore the world of Oaxacan alebrijes, wacky and vibrant wooden sculptures crafted by hand. Explore the many artisan workshops in Oaxaca, especially in Arrazola and San Martin Tilcajete, where talented artisans create these amazing animals. Every alebrije is a one-of-a-kind work of art that embodies the vivid essence of Oaxacan culture as well as the artist's inventiveness.

Textiles and Weaving: The Art of Zapotec Tradition

Location: Teotitlan del Valle, Oaxaca, Mexico

The rich weaving history of Teotitlan del Valle welcomes you to discover the artistry of Zapotec textiles. Visit neighborhood workshops where skilled weavers create exquisite blankets, rugs, and clothing using age-old methods. Admire the skillful transformation of raw materials into breathtaking textile creations, as well as the use of natural dyes made from plants and insects.

Black Pottery of San Bartolo Coyotepec

Location: San Bartolo Coyotepec, Oaxaca, Mexico

Famous for its distinctive black pottery, which is made from a particular kind of clay and polished to a glossy sheen, is San Bartolo Coyotepec. Discover the workshops where the artists create these unique pieces by shaping, molding, and firing them in this little hamlet. In addition to being aesthetically arresting, San Bartolo Coyotepec's black pottery offers evidence of the region's long-standing ceramic traditions.

Local Souvenirs: Treasures to Carry Home

Mezcal: Spirit of Oaxaca

Enjoy mezcal, the distinctive spirit of Oaxacan culture, and take a piece of Oaxacan culture home with you. Visit some of the area's mezcalarias to see how agave is traditionally fermented and distilled to create this unique liquor. Get a bottle of handcrafted mezcal to remember your trip by, and enjoy the tastes of Oaxaca for years to come.

Oaxacan Chocolate: Sweet Memories

Rich and velvety chocolate is Oaxaca's specialty, and it's a cuisines that's firmly embedded in the region's cultural legacy. Visit Oaxaca City's chocolate establishments, like Mayordomo, to see how chocolate is traditionally made with stone milletes. To bring the flavors of Oaxaca's chocolate-making culture into your house, buy chocolate bars, cocoa powder, or hot chocolate mix.

Huipils and Embroidery: Wearable Art

Get yourself a traditional huipil, an exquisitely embroidered blouse worn by indigenous women, to totally immerse yourself in Oaxacan fashion. In Oaxaca City and the surrounding communities, visit markets and artisan cooperatives to discover huipils embellished with elaborate designs that pay homage to the Zapotec people's rich cultural legacy. These adornable works of art provide thoughtful and fashionable mementos.

Navigating Oaxaca's Markets and Shopping Districts

Mercado de Artesanías de Oaxaca: Artisan Market

Address: Mercado de Artesanías de Oaxaca, Calle de Rayón, Centro, Oaxaca, Mexico **Latitude:** 17.0651° N **Longitude:** 96.7267° W

Discover the Mercado de Artesanías de Oaxaca, a specialized artisan market offering a wide assortment of handcrafted items and mementos. This market provides an array of well-chosen examples of Oaxacan workmanship, ranging from jewelry and leather goods to textiles and ceramics. Interact with craftspeople, discover how they come up with their ideas, and bring home one-of-a-kind finds.

Andador Macedonio Alcalá: Shopping Promenade

Location: Andador Macedonio Alcalá, Oaxaca, Mexico

Take a stroll down Oaxaca City's lovely promenade, the Andador Macedonio Alcalá, which is dotted with artisan stores, galleries, and boutiques. This pedestrian-only strip is a great place to discover fashion, contemporary art, and unusual treasures. Savor a relaxed shopping experience while interacting with local vendors and finding hidden treasures.

Pochote Market: Sustainable and Local

Address: Pochote Market, Calle de Alcalá, Centro, Oaxaca, Mexico **Latitude:** 17.0644° N **Longitude:** 96.7248° W

A must-visit for anyone looking for locally sourced and sustainable products is the Pochote Market. This market offers a variety of organic fruit, handcrafted goods, and artisanal crafts, with an emphasis on fair trade and eco-friendly practices. Enjoy a sustainable and ethical market experience while supporting your neighborhood's farmers and craftsmen.

Practical Tips for Enjoyable Shopping Adventures

Bargaining Etiquette

Shop at the markets of Oaxaca and follow the custom of haggling. Although there are certain places with set prices, haggling is a typical activity, particularly in artisan marketplaces. Remember that the aim of negotiations is to arrive at a reasonable and agreeable price, and conduct yourself with friendliness and respect throughout the process.

Cash and Local Currency

When visiting smaller markets and making purchases from street vendors, it's best to have cash in Mexican pesos, however some larger institutions and markets may accept credit cards. Oaxaca City has a large number of ATMs for easy money exchange.

Language Considerations

Even though many artists and vendors, particularly in tourist-oriented regions, may speak some Basic English, knowing a few

Spanish phrases might help you communicate effectively. Acquiring proficiency in a few essential phrases will improve your shopping encounters and encourage goodwill relationships with local vendors.

Conclusion: Oaxaca's Shopping Shades Unveiled

You join the lively weaves of Oaxacan trade as you explore the busy Mercado Benito Juarez, go on creative excursions through the city's crafts, and bring home regional mementos that weave stories of history. Every trip to the market, every interaction with an artisan, and every purchase all help to preserve and honor Oaxaca's rich creative and cultural legacy.

May your shopping finds act as physical reminders of the hues, tastes, and artistry that characterize Oaxaca as you carry them. Every object becomes a window into the spirit of this fascinating place, whether it's the rich needlework of a huipil, the vivid colors of an alebrije, or the earthy scent of Oaxacan chocolate.

As you bid adieu to Oaxaca's marketplaces and retail areas, remember the tales enshrouded in the textiles, the hands that mold the clay, and the lively energy of a people proud of its creative heritage. ¡Viva la culture y el arte de Oaxaca! (Long live Oaxaca's art and culture!)

Extended Shopping Excursions: Beyond the Markets

San Pedro Taviche: Mezcal Exploration

Go beyond the usual markets and discover San Pedro Taviche, a hamlet known for making mezcal. This community, which is close to Oaxaca City, provides a rare chance to see the whole mezcal-making process in action. Visit the nearby palenques, or mezcal distillery, where master mezcaleros create this popular Oaxacan alcoholic beverage. Buy handcrafted mezcal straight from the makers; each bottle reveals a tale of skill and heritage.

Village Pottery Studios: Discovering Artisanal Excellence

Set off on a trip to communities known for their unique ceramic traditions to begin your pottery journey. Visit the Atzompa village, which is known for its green-glazed ceramics, or go to San Marcos Tlapazola for black pottery. See the artists at work as they mold, paint, and fire their creations. This is your chance to purchase one-of-a-kind items straight from the creators.

Tejate and Traditional Sweets: Culinary Souvenirs

Discover the food scene in Oaxaca outside of Mercado Benito Juarez. Look for neighborhood confectioneries that sell classic sweets like nicuatole (a sweet corn pudding), alegrías (amaranth and honey bars), and molletes (canned sweet potatoes). Don't pass up the opportunity to have tejate, a pre-Hispanic drink prepared with cacao and maize that is frequently decorated with elaborate designs. These delectable mementos capture the essence of Oaxaca's rich gastronomic history.

Immersive Artisan Experiences: Workshops and Classes

Alebrijes Painting Workshops

Location: Various Artisan Studios, Oaxaca, Mexico

Take advantage of the painting classes that neighborhood artists are offering to fully immerse yourself in the world of alebrijes. You can use your imagination to bring an unpainted alebrije to life with these interactive experiences. Discover the meaning of the patterns and methods employed in alebrijes, and make a unique work of Oaxacan art to bring home.

Textile Weaving Classes in Teotitlan del Valle

Location: Teotitlan del Valle, Oaxaca, Mexico

Enroll in textile weaving courses in Teotitlan del Valle to learn more about the craft of Zapotec weaving. Collaborate with proficient weavers to comprehend the complex procedure involved in producing vivid textiles. Select your hues, get proficient in age-old weaving methods, and create a miniature cloth as a sentimental memento of your artistic sojourn in Oaxaca.

Mezcal Tasting and Blending Sessions

Location: Mezcalarias in Oaxaca, Mexico

Take part in the mezcalarias' tasting and mixing sessions to develop a deeper appreciation for mezcal. Discover the many agave cultivars, distillation techniques, and flavor characteristics. With the help of professionals, craft your own mezcal mix and learn about the craft of mezcal manufacturing. Take with you a personalized bottle that perfectly encapsulates your mezcal experience.

Sustainable Shopping Practices: Ethical Souvenir Hunting

Supporting Artisan Cooperatives

Make the decision to assist artisan collectives and cooperatives that place a high priority on sustainable practices and fair salaries. Numerous cooperatives work to protect traditional crafts while guaranteeing the welfare of their members. When making purchases, seek out certification or signs of fair trade standards to support the long-term viability of Oaxaca's artisanal traditions.

Eco-Friendly Souvenirs

Choose souvenirs that are sustainable and made of eco-friendly materials. Choose products that are made from repurposed or recycled materials to lessen the impact of your purchases on the environment. Selecting eco-friendly mementos, such as reusable textiles and recycled glassware, is consistent with Oaxaca's dedication to protecting its natural beauty.

Cultural Respect in Artisanal Encounters

Be mindful of the cultural differences in your interactions with sellers and craftspeople. Spend some time learning about the cultural background and significance of the crafts that are being made. A craftsperson's work may lose value if you force them to drastically reduce their costs. By encouraging polite conversations, you help to keep Oaxaca's cultural legacy alive.

Conclusion: Your Oaxacan Shopping Saga

As you wrap up your Oaxacan shopping adventure, consider the wide range of finds you've made and the cross-cultural relationships you've formed. Every piece narrates a tale of customs, artistry, and the colorful essence of Oaxaca. Your mementos, whether they be a bottle of handcrafted mezcal, a hand-painted alebrije, or a weaves woven using traditional methods, are more than just trinkets; they are windows into Oaxaca's spirit.

The core of your journey is not just in the material objects you carry, but also in the intangible experiences that have deepened your understanding of Oaxacan culture. Keep this in mind as you pack your carefully selected items and say goodbye to Oaxaca's markets. I hope your mementos will act as a constant reminder of the vivid hues, mouthwatering cuisine, and creative heritage that make Oaxaca an enduring destination for travelers wishing to explore its diverse cultural landscape. ¡Viva Oaxaca's creativity and craftsmanship! (Long live Oaxaca's workmanship and art!)

Celebrating Oaxaca's Cultural weaves: A Deep Dive into Festivals and Events (2024-2025)

Introduction: Oaxaca's Vibrant Shades of Festivals

Take a cultural tour of Oaxaca, a place where festivity permeates every aspect of daily existence. We examine additional yearly events that highlight the diversity of Oaxaca's culture in this extensive guide, including the legendary Guelaguetza Festival and the captivating Day of the Dead celebrations. Discover the maps, addresses, and coordinates that will lead you right into the center of Oaxaca's colorful traditions as we make our way through these events.

Guelaguetza Festival: The Dance of Cultural Harmony

Overview of the Guelaguetza Festival

The Guelaguetza Festival, also known as "Los Lunes del Cerro" or "Mondays on the Hill," is one of the most important and representative holidays in Oaxaca. This indigenous cultural celebration, which takes place every July, brings together communities from all around the state to demonstrate their traditional dances, music, costumes, and food.

Venue: Auditorio Guelaguetza

Address: Auditorio Guelaguetza, Calle de Ignacio Rayón, Cerro del Fortín, Oaxaca, Mexico **Latitude:** 17.0656° N **Longitude:** 96.7191° W

Situated atop the Cerro del Fortín hill, the famous Auditorio Guelaguetza hosts the Guelaguetza Festival. This outdoor amphitheater offers a panoramic backdrop for the cultural event, enabling thousands of attendees to see the colorful acts against Oaxaca City's picturesque scenery.

The Dance of the Guelaguetza: A Symbolic Performance

The "Danza de la Guelaguetza," a symbolic dance that personifies the idea of community and sharing, is the focal point of the Guelaguetza Festival. Dancers with elaborate choreographies that tell tales of Oaxaca's indigenous past are dressed in vibrant traditional garb. A captivating weaves of cultural expression is woven together by the lively colors of costumes, the melodies of traditional instruments, and the rhythmic beats of drums.

Cuisines: Tasting Oaxaca's Flavors

The Guelaguetza is a feast for the senses in addition to being an impressive sight. The "Feria del Mezcal y de la Gastronomía," the festival's food fair, highlights Oaxaca's illustrious culinary history. Taste traditional fare like tlayudas, mole, and chapulines, all paired with the famous mezcal, a drink that is closely associated with Oaxacan culture.

Day of the Dead Celebrations: Honoring Ancestral Spirits

Overview of Day of the Dead in Oaxaca

"Día de los Muertos," or Day of the Dead, celebrations in Oaxaca go beyond simple remembering; they are a lively proclamation of life and a deep bond with ancestor spirits. This multi-day celebration, which runs from October 31 to November 2, blends Catholic and indigenous customs to create a singular and strikingly beautiful remembrance.

Cemeteries and Altars: A weaves of Remembrance

Location: Various Cemeteries in Oaxaca, Mexico

Families come together at graves all throughout Oaxaca on the Day of the Dead to pay respects to their deceased loved ones. Panteón General is one of the most famous cemeteries, where ornately decorated graves serve as focal points for candles, marigolds, and donations. In order to create a weaves of remembrance, altars, also known as "ofrendas," are erected in homes and public areas and decorated with pictures, beloved foods, and sentimental items.

Processions and Comparsas: Communal Celebrations

Take in the colorful comparsas (parades) and processions that liven up Oaxaca's streets on the Day of the Dead. Face painting, music, and elaborate costumes all add to the joyous atmosphere. Locals gather to celebrate, and processions frequently end at cemeteries where people gather to enjoy meals, exchange tales, and relive cherished memories.

Sand Shades: Intricate Alfombras de Arena

Location: Various Streets and Plazas in Oaxaca, Mexico

Discover how the Day of the Dead is portrayed artistically with "alfombras de arena" (sand weaves). On sidewalks and plazas, skilled craftspeople and locals use dyed sawdust or sand to create elaborate and vibrant designs. These transient pieces of art feature religious themes, traditional symbols, and settings that allude to the cyclical nature of life and death.

Other Annual Events: A Calendar of

Cultural Highlights

Oaxaca FilmFest: Celebrating Cinematic Excellence

Venue: Various Locations in Oaxaca, Mexico **Latitude and Longitude:** Coordinates Vary by Venue

A celebration of independent cinema from around the globe, the Oaxaca FilmFest takes place every year in a variety of venues around Oaxaca, including historic theaters and cultural spaces. Film enthusiasts, industry professionals, and filmmakers come together for this event, which offers a wide range of films, panel discussions, and a celebration of the craft of cinematic storytelling.

Noche de Rábanos: Radish Carving Extravaganza

Location: Zócalo, Oaxaca, Mexico **Latitude:** 17.0656° N **Longitude:** 96.7236° W

The unique and beloved custom known as Noche de Rábanos, or Night of the Radishes, is celebrated on December 23 at Oaxaca's Zócalo. Giant radishes are carved into elaborate sculptures by local artists, showcasing their artistic talent. The occasion draws both locals and tourists since it provides a joyous setting with food, music, and the opportunity to take in the striking artworks created by radish artists.

Festival de la Ciudad: Oaxaca's Birthday Celebration

Venue: Various Locations in Oaxaca, Mexico **Latitude and Longitude:** Coordinates Vary by Venue

Oaxaca celebrates its founding anniversary with a number of cultural activities and performances known as the Festival de la Ciudad. This festival, which takes place all around the city, pays tribute to Oaxaca's artistic accomplishments, history, and customs. Concerts, dances, art shows, and other events that highlight the dynamic cultural identity of the city are available to visitors.

Navigating Oaxaca's Festivals: Practical Tips

Guelaguetza Festival Attendance Tips

To guarantee a spot at the Auditorio Guelaguetza, if you intend to attend the Guelaguetza Festival, think about buying tickets in advance. Get there early to take in the pre-festival festivities and peruse the food fair. The event is held outdoors, so dress comfortably and pack for a range of weather scenarios.

Day of the Dead Participation Guidelines

Participating in the Day of the Dead festivities with respect is essential. When visiting graves, stay back and don't interfere with families having private rites. Keep in consideration local customs and act with respect when participating in processions or making sand weaves. Engage in the celebration with reverence and an awareness of its importance.

Other Annual Events Logistics

Make sure to verify the official schedule and venue details ahead of time for events such as the Oaxaca FilmFest. If you need tickets, get them and check out the variety of films available. When attending Noche de Rábanos and Festival de la Ciudad, get there early to get a good spot. You should also think about joining in on the fun by eating traditional meals and mingling with the locals.

Conclusion: Weaving Memories in Oaxaca's Cultural Shades

You become a part of a living cultural weaves as you take in the vibrant Guelaguetza Festival performances, marvel at the elaborate sand weaves on Day of the Dead, and get involved in the many activities that fill Oaxaca's calendar. Every celebration and occasion adds to Oaxaca's lively and rich identity, acting as a unifying theme.

Take with you the memories of dancing, music, art, and group celebrations as you wrap up your tour of Oaxaca's festivals and festivities. May the experiences you gain in Oaxaca become enduring threads in your own weaves of memories, and may the addresses and coordinates lead you to the center of each cultural show. ¡Viva la tradición y fiestas oaxaca! (Long live Oaxaca's festivities and culture!)

Extended Cultural Explorations: Seasonal Highlights

Monte Albán Light and Sound Show

Location: Monte Albán Archaeological Site, Oaxaca, Mexico
Latitude: 17.0431° N **Longitude:** 96.7674° W

Attend the exciting Monte Albán Light and Sound Show, an evening event hosted at the historic Monte Albán archaeological site, to extend your cultural adventures. A multimedia presentation that tells the story of the secrets and history of this UNESCO World Heritage site takes place as evening descends over the Zapotec ruins. Your Oaxacan cultural trip gains an additional layer thanks to the captivating journey through time created by the combination of light, music, and narration.

Semana Santa: Holy Week Celebrations

Various Locations in Oaxaca, Mexico Latitude and Longitude: Coordinates Vary by Venue

Discover the rich religious and cultural customs of Oaxaca during Semana Santa, often known as Holy Week. The city and neighboring settlements host a variety of processions, religious celebrations, and artistic events. Take in the elaborate alfombras (street carpets), religious imagery, and general reverent atmosphere as both locals and tourists gather to commemorate this momentous week in the Catholic calendar.

Night of the Radishes Extended Celebrations

The creative mood goes beyond the radish carvings, however Noche de Rábanos is undoubtedly the highlight. Take advantage of the extended festivities in the days preceding Christmas Eve, such as craft fairs, art exhibits, and dining occasions. Interact with regional artists who demonstrate skills beyond carving radish to gain a greater understanding of the variety of artistic expression that Oaxaca has to offer throughout the holiday season.

Immersive Cultural Workshops: Participation in Tradition

Guelaguetza Dance Workshops

Location: Various Dance Studios in Oaxaca, Mexico **Latitude and Longitude:** Coordinates Vary by Venue

Take advantage of the Guelaguetza's colorful traditions by enrolling in dance classes taught by native teachers. Discover the complex motions, steps, and meanings associated with the dances performed at the event. These classes offer a deeper connection to Oaxaca's indigenous heritage by offering not only a physical experience but also insights into the cultural significance of each dance.

Day of the Dead Altar-Making Classes

Location: Cultural Centers and Workshops in Oaxaca, Mexico **Latitude and Longitude:** Coordinates Vary by Venue

Take part in lessons on creating altars for the Day of the Dead to get a hands-on understanding of the cultural customs surrounding this moving holiday. Workshops where you may learn the symbolic elements, skills, and personal touches that go into producing an ofrenda are frequently offered by local artists and cultural centers. Making your personal altar is a deeply moving way to pay tribute to the deceased and add to the memorial's common fabric.

Mezcal Tasting and Artisanal Crafts Sessions

Location: Mezcalarias and Artisan Studios in Oaxaca, Mexico
Latitude and Longitude: Coordinates Vary by Venue

Through intensive courses, explore the craftsmanship of mezcal production and traditional crafts. Attend mezcal tastings conducted by master mezcaleros who will share their expertise on distillation, fermentation, and agave varietals. Take part in artisanal craft workshops as well, where regional artisans teach you how to make your own Oaxacan masterpiece by teaching you techniques like weaving, pottery, or alebrije painting.

Sustainable Engagement in Cultural Celebrations

Responsible Tourism Practices

Use responsible tourism strategies when attending workshops and cultural events. Please heed any instructions given by the organizers, respect the cultural significance of rites and traditions, and ask permission before taking any pictures. Reduce your environmental effect while making a positive contribution to the communities you interact with by patronizing nearby companies and artists.

Cultural Exchange and Dialogue

Talk to locals and other participants in order to facilitate cultural interaction. Share your own cultural heritage, ask polite questions, and attend community events with an open mind. Engage in discussions that foster respect and understanding between people to contribute to a rich exchange of viewpoints while you are immersed in Oaxaca culture.

Sustainable Souvenirs and Artisan Support

When making workshop purchases or souvenir purchases, give preference to products made sustainably and responsibly. Give support to craftspeople who follow fair trade and environmentally responsible techniques. Select mementos that support the local economy and the preservation of traditional craftsmanship, in line with your personal beliefs.

Conclusion: A Cultural Odyssey Unveiled

As you broaden your cultural investigations to encompass immersive workshops, seasonal highlights, and responsible participation, your trip to Oaxaca transforms into a cultural odyssey—a mosaic of encounters interwoven with elements of dance, art, and customs. In addition to being physical landmarks, the addresses and coordinates supplied open doors to more meaningful interactions and help visitors have a greater understanding of the daily customs that characterize Oaxacan culture.

Bring the inventiveness of Noche de Rábanos, the respect of Day of the Dead, and the spirit of Guelaguetza with you as you wrap out your cultural journey. I hope that the experiences you had attending seminars and long festivities will get woven into the fabric of your own cultural identity. May the cultural fabric you've absorbed create a lasting connection to the lively customs of this enchanted region as you say goodbye to Oaxaca. ¡Viva la tradición y culture de Oaxaca! (Long live Oaxaca's culture and traditions!)

Oaxaca Nights: A Comprehensive Guide to Nightlife and Entertainment (2024-2025)

Introduction: Unveiling the Nocturnal Charms of Oaxaca

In this comprehensive guide, we navigate through the labyrinth of bars and clubs, groove to the beat of live music venues, and immerse ourselves in the cultural performances that define Oaxaca's after-hours scene. Follow the maps, discover the addresses, and embrace the coordinates that lead you to the heart of Oaxaca's nightlife and entertainment. As the sun sets over the colonial streets of Oaxaca, a vibrant nocturnal energy comes to life, beckoning tourists and locals alike to explore the city's varied and lively nightlife.

Bars and Clubs: A Spectrum of Nocturnal Delights

Zandunga Bar

Address: Calle 5 de Mayo 312, Centro, Oaxaca, Mexico **Latitude:** 17.0639° N **Longitude:** 96.7246° W

Start your nighttime adventure with Zandunga Bar, a cultural hotspot tucked away in the Centro neighborhood of Oaxaca. With a wide variety of this legendary liquor, this bar is a celebration of mezcal. Enjoy well-made mezcal cocktails and discover the many flavors of this iconic Oaxacan beverage while taking in the cozy atmosphere filled with traditional Oaxacan décor.

La Mezcalerita

Address: Calle de M. Bravo 210, Centro, Oaxaca, Mexico
Latitude: 17.0645° N **Longitude:** 96.7226° W

Explore La Mezcalerita's diverse atmosphere, a modern mezcaleria that blends traditional and modern aspects. This bar, which is situated in the center of Oaxaca's historic district, serves inventive drinks that highlight the versatility of mezcal in addition to a carefully chosen assortment of the recognized spirit. La Mezcalerita is a vibrant option for a night out because of its live music events and energetic patrons.

Bar Fly Oaxaca

Address: Calle de Miguel Hidalgo 706, Centro, Oaxaca, Mexico
Latitude: 17.0618° N **Longitude:** 96.7219° W

Bar Fly Oaxaca is waiting for anyone looking for a blend of classic cocktails and modern ambiance. This chic, urban-themed restaurant has a broad drink menu that extends beyond mezcal, including creative cocktails, beers, and spirits from around the world. For an elegant night out, Bar Fly Oaxaca is a top choice because of its stylish atmosphere and sporadic DJ sets.

Biblioteca Bar

Address: Calle de M. Bravo 210B, Centro, Oaxaca, Mexico
Latitude: 17.0650° N **Longitude:** 96.7248° W

Take in the creative and intellectual atmosphere of Biblioteca Bar, which is next to the Santo Domingo church. This distinctive location offers a selection of drinks inspired by literary classics, fusing the passion of books with mixology. Sip your drink in the book-lined, comfortable atmosphere or take a breather on the courtyard.

Latitude 17 Rooftop Bar

Address: Hotel Casa Oaxaca, Calle de Xicoténcatl 312, Centro, Oaxaca, Mexico **Latitude:** 17.0635° N **Longitude:** 96.7227° W

Experience nightlife to the fullest at Hotel Casa Oaxaca's Latitude 17 Rooftop Bar. This chic rooftop bar provides expansive views of the Santo Domingo church and the city skyline. Savor handcrafted drinks, take in the refreshing breeze, and take in the alluring atmosphere that elevates Latitude 17 to the status of a must-visit location for an unforgettable evening.

Live Music Venues: The Soundtrack of Oaxacan Nights

Casa de la Ciudad

Address: Reforma 506, Centro, Oaxaca, Mexico **Latitude:** 17.0631° N **Longitude:** 96.7236° W

Enter Casa de la Ciudad, a cultural oasis where live music is a main attraction. From modern genres to traditional Oaxacan tunes, a range of musical acts take place in this ancient theater. See the event calendar for upcoming events to make sure you don't miss an engaging live show in a small, ethnically diverse venue.

Café Central

Address: Avenida 5 de Mayo 208, Centro, Oaxaca, Mexico **Latitude:** 17.0634° N **Longitude:** 96.7227° W

Tucked down in the core of Oaxaca's historic district, Café Central is a bustling live music venue in addition to being a coffee heaven. Jazz, blues, and traditional Oaxacan music are just a few of the many genres that are played at Café Central, which offers a relaxed atmosphere and excellent artists to enjoy while you sip your favorite drink.

El Zaguán

Address: Calle de Macedonio Alcalá 518, Centro, Oaxaca, Mexico **Latitude:** 17.0625° N **Longitude:** 96.7251° W

Discover the cozy beauty of El Zaguán, a cultural venue that presents artistic performances, poetry readings, and live music events. For music lovers, this venue—tucked away in a historic building—offers a genuine and comfortable environment. For jazz evenings, acoustic sessions, and other musical delights that enhance Oaxaca's nightlife, check their program.

Candela Roots Bar

Address: Avenida Independencia 1007, Centro, Oaxaca, Mexico **Latitude:** 17.0632° N **Longitude:** 96.7222° W

Candela Roots Bar calls to anyone looking for Latin beats, salsa, and reggae rhythms. This vibrant establishment, which is situated on Avenida Independencia, has DJ sets and live bands that keep the dance floor packed. Take in the lively ambiance, where a unique experience is created by the blending of music and culture.

Cultural Performances: Theatrical and Artistic Extravaganzas

Teatro Macedonio Alcalá

Address: Calle de Macedonio Alcalá 403, Centro, Oaxaca, Mexico **Latitude:** 17.0617° N **Longitude:** 96.7256° W

In the center of Oaxaca, there is a cultural gem called Teatro Macedonio Alcalá. Enter its splendor. A range of cultural events, including as ballet recitals, classical concerts, and theater productions, are presented at this ancient theater. Examine the program for forthcoming events and become fully immersed in Oaxaca's rich artistic legacy within the elaborate walls of this legendary location.

Centro Cultural San Pablo

Address: Calle de Independencia 507, Centro, Oaxaca, Mexico
Latitude: 17.0643° N **Longitude:** 96.7230° W

Discover the vibrant arts scene at Centro Cultural San Pablo, a multipurpose venue that presents live concerts, workshops, and art exhibitions. This cultural hub displays the range of Oaxaca's artistic expression, from experimental theater to modern dance. Come to a show and interact with the neighborhood's artistic community in this thriving cultural center.

Plaza de la Danza

Address: Calle de M. Bravo, Centro, Oaxaca, Mexico **Latitude:** 17.0634° N **Longitude:** 96.7233° W

Discover the enchantment of outdoor cultural events at Plaza de la Danza. Theater, music, and traditional dance are presented on this ancient square. The Plaza de la Danza, surrounded by Oaxaca's rich cultural heritage and colonial architecture, provides an engrossing environment in which to observe the creative weaves that takes shape beneath the night sky.

Navigating Oaxaca's Nightlife: Practical Tips

Mezcal Tasting Etiquette

Accept the local practice of sipping mezcal slowly and enjoying its flavors when visiting mezcalerias. Talk to the experienced employees to find out more about the various types and manufacturing processes. Take part in mezcal tastings to learn more about this known Oaxacan alcoholic beverage.

Live Music Schedule Planning

To organize your evenings, check the schedules of live music venues and cultural spaces ahead of time. You may be sure to catch your favorite form of music because many places host special evenings featuring particular genres. For popular shows, especially in smaller venues, get there early to get a good spot and take in the cozy environment.

Cultural Event Ticketing

If you're going to a theater or other cultural event, think about getting tickets in advance, especially for popular plays. Make sure you don't miss out on any future events by checking with cultural institutions and venues about upcoming plays, dance performances, and art exhibitions. Encourage local artists and add to the rich cultural landscape of Oaxaca.

Conclusion: Nocturnal Oaxacan Symphony

You join Oaxaca's nighttime orchestra as you explore the mezcal-filled bars, dance to live music that reverberates through the city's historic streets, and take in cultural events that take place outside. Not only do the maps, addresses, and coordinates help with travel, but they also serve as doors to the city's creative and rhythmic core.

As you get to the end of your investigation of Oaxaca's entertainment options, may your senses be left with memories of nights filled with mezcal, dreams of live music, and cultural spectacles. When you say goodbye to Oaxaca's magical evenings, take with you the sounds of laughing, the resonance of songs, and the vivid colors of cultural expressions that characterize the city's attraction after dark. ¡Viva la culture y la viva nocturna de Oaxaca! (Long live Oaxaca's nightlife and culture!)

Extended Nightlife Experiences: Hidden

Gems and Late-Night Delights

Expendio Tradición

Address: Calle de García Vigil 104, Centro, Oaxaca, Mexico
Latitude: 17.0638° N **Longitude:** 96.7265° W

Visit Expendio Tradición to take a tour through the center of Oaxaca's cultural scene. This undiscovered gem skillfully combines modern art with traditional mezcal experiences. For lovers of mezcal, the exposed brick walls with their displays of regional art create a cozy atmosphere. Come in late to beat the crowds and take in the relaxed ambiance while perusing their extensive assortment of mezcal.

Las Quince Letras

Address: Calle de M. Bravo 519, Centro, Oaxaca, Mexico
Latitude: 17.0623° N **Longitude:** 96.7251° W

Savor the sophisticated atmosphere of Las Quince Letras, a restaurant and mezcalería that has a captivating aura that carries over into the evening. This establishment, which is housed in a historic building, is known for its delicious food and mezcal expertise. A sophisticated audience arrives in the evening, which makes it the perfect place for a late-night mezcal tasting accompanied with Oaxacan cuisine.

El Candil Bar

Address: Calle de Macedonio Alcalá 104, Centro, Oaxaca, Mexico **Latitude:** 17.0623° N **Longitude:** 96.7267° W

Visit El Candil Bar for a taste of tradition mixed with modern flair. This bar, tucked away in the center of Oaxaca's artists sector, serves a variety of artisan cocktails and mezcals. With its cozy ambiance and tasteful art displays, the small venue is the perfect place to spend a long evening with friends or other travelers.

Cine-Club El Pochote

Address: Calle de M. Bravo 408, Centro, Oaxaca, Mexico
Latitude: 17.0618° N **Longitude:** 96.7261° W

Enjoy the distinctive fusion of nightlife and film at Cine-Club El Pochote. This cultural venue hosts talks, film screenings, and activities that frequently go late. Take in the indie film scene and engage in cross-cultural conversation while having a fun, alternative evening in Oaxaca.

Nightlife beyond the Centro: Exploring Oaxaca's Districts

Colonia Reforma: Calle Allende Strip

Address: Calle Allende, Colonia Reforma, Oaxaca, Mexico
Latitude and Longitude: Coordinates Vary Along Calle Allende

Enter the hip Colonia Reforma neighborhood and discover the exciting nightlife on Calle Allende. Locals and tourists congregate at this strip's many pubs, clubs, and restaurants for a varied evening of entertainment. There is something for every nighttime partygoer on the Allende Strip, from vibrant bars to dancing clubs.

Jalatlaco: Bohemian Nights

Address: Calle de Manuel Ruiz 200, Jalatlaco, Oaxaca, Mexico
Latitude: 17.0630° N **Longitude:** 96.7195° W

Experience Jalatlaco's bohemian appeal; this area is known for its distinctive vibe and creative energy. Discover neighborhood tucked-away amid colonial courtyards bars and mezcalerías. Jalatlaco is the perfect neighborhood for a leisurely evening of exploration and cultural interactions because of its laid-back atmosphere and creative vibes.

Xochimilco: Riverside Rhythms

Address: Calzada de la República, Xochimilco, Oaxaca, Mexico
Latitude: 17.0666° N **Longitude:** 96.7218° W

Explore the allure of Xochimilco's riverbank, where events take place along the Calzada de la República at night. Discover the restaurants and pubs by the Atoyac River that offer a distinctive atmosphere. For a more relaxed and beautiful night out, the serene surroundings, softly lit by lights reflecting on the water, make a stunning backdrop.

Safety and Responsible Nightlife Practices

Local Customs and Respectful Behavior

Participating in Oaxaca's nightlife requires respecting regional traditions and manners. Oaxacan culture values polite behavior, so pay attention to your surroundings and treat people, both locals and other revelers, with respect. This adds to a pleasant and inviting evening scene in addition to improving your individual experience.

Transportation and Navigation

Make sure your evening outings have safe transportation options. When traveling between neighborhoods or going back to your lodging, think about utilizing trustworthy taxi services or ridesharing applications. Pay attention to your surroundings and stick to busy, well-lit places, especially when venturing into neighborhoods outside of the Centro.

Responsible Consumption of Mezcal and Beverages

Savor Oaxaca's famous mezcal in moderation. Take it slow, enjoy the tastes, and know your boundaries. It's critical to drink plenty of water and limit alcohol intake. In addition to keeping you safe, responsible drinking enables you to completely enjoy the myriad flavors and cultural significance of Oaxaca's popular mezcal.

Conclusion: Oaxaca's Nocturnal Shades Unveiled

You become a part of a nighttime weaves as you make your way through the prolonged experiences, varied districts, and undiscovered treasures that make up Oaxaca's nightlife. Here are the maps, locations, and coordinates to help you discover the city's hidden charms after hours. As you wrap up your nighttime discovery of Oaxaca, may the melodies of live performances, the rhythms of mezcal-infused nights, and the cultural spectacles remain as colorful threads in your voyage through the night.

When you say goodbye to Oaxaca's magical evenings, take with you the sounds of laughing, the resonance of songs, and the vivid colors of cultural expressions that characterize the city's attraction after dark. ¡Viva la culture y la viva nocturna de Oaxaca! (Long live Oaxaca's nightlife and culture!)

Late-Night Eateries: Cuisines under the Moonlight

Tlayudas under the Stars

Address: Calle de las Casas 101, Centro, Oaxaca, Mexico
Latitude: 17.0654° N **Longitude:** 96.7242° W

Treat yourself some tlayudas, a traditional Oaxacan treat, to satisfy your late-night desires. For a real experience, visit the street merchants on Calle de las Casas. Savor large, crispy tortillas topped with a flavorful mixture of beans, cheese, meats, and avocado while the moon shines. These alfresco dining establishments offer a relaxed and delectable end to your evening adventures.

Street Taquerías in La Merced

Address: Calle de J.P. García 406, La Merced, Oaxaca, Mexico
Latitude: 17.0658° N **Longitude:** 96.7245° W

Discover the tastes of the La Merced neighborhood's street food scene in Oaxaca. Local taquerías come alive as the night goes on, serving a variety of tacos with vivid toppings, fresh salsas, and exquisite meats. Savor the many flavors of Oaxacan street food beneath the stars with the natives.

Chocolate Caliente at Mercado Benito Juarez

Address: Calle de Rayón, Centro, Oaxaca, Mexico **Latitude:** 17.0652° N **Longitude:** 96.7217° W

Stop into Mercado Benito Juarez for a cup of authentic Oaxacan hot chocolate to cap off your midnight explorations with something delicious and cozy. In the late evening, the market comes to life and provides a comfortable setting for savoring the rich, velvety warmth of chocolate caliente. For a delicious midnight treat, pair it with sweet bread or locally made pastries.

Nighttime Strolls: Embracing Oaxaca's Ambiance after Dark

Alameda de León: Serene Nighttime Retreat

Address: Calle de José María Pino Suárez, Centro, Oaxaca, Mexico **Latitude:** 17.0647° N **Longitude:** 96.7198° W

Take a leisurely stroll through Alameda de León to cap off your evening. After dusk, this charming park assumes a calm atmosphere that offers a peaceful escape from the busy streets. In Oaxaca's central park, take in the serene and contemplative ambiance while seeing the lit fountains, statues, and surrounding colonial buildings.

Templo de Santo Domingo: Illuminated Majesty

Address: Calle de Macedonio Alcalá, Centro, Oaxaca, Mexico
Latitude: 17.0637° N **Longitude:** 96.7241° W

Take in the charm of Templo de Santo Domingo at night, when it transforms into a regal beacon. In the solitude of the night, this architectural marvel acquires a new charm. End your nighttime exploration with a leisurely stroll around the church, photographing the minute details lit up against the night sky.

Responsible Nighttime Exploration: A Considerate Farewell

Waste Reduction and Eco-Friendly Practices

When you go on your nocturnal travels, keep eco-friendly and waste-reduction activities in mind. For street food, use reusable containers; stay away from single-use plastics; and dispose of waste properly. Keeping Oaxaca's streets clean guarantees a good and long-lasting nighttime experience for all.

Safety Precautions during Late-Night Strolls

Prioritize safety when taking pleasure in nocturnal strolls by staying on well-traveled paths and well-lit areas. When at all feasible, go in groups and pay attention to your surroundings. In order to guarantee a safe and enjoyable experience when exploring the city after dark, abide by any municipal curfews or safety regulations.

Gratitude for Oaxaca's Nighttime Magic

Give thanks for the special and enchanting experiences Oaxaca has to offer after dark. All of your nighttime experiences in Oaxaca contribute to the rich weaves of memories you will have, whether you choose to indulge in late-night street cuisine, dance to live music in energetic venues, or sip mezcal in secret mezcalerías.

Conclusion: Oaxaca's Nocturnal Symphony

As you come to the end of your midnight tour of Oaxaca, from secret mezcalerías to late-night taquerías and peaceful strolls across the city, may the sounds of street food, laughing, and the ethereal atmosphere of Oaxaca's nightly symphony be with you forever. Take with you the memories of moonlit streets, bustling plazas, and the colorful weaves of experiences that characterize Oaxaca after dark as you bid adieu to the city's nocturnal enchantment. ¡Viva la magia y la viva nocturna en Oaxaca! (Long live Oaxaca's nightlife and magic!)

Navigating Oaxaca with Grace: A Comprehensive Guide to Local Tips and Etiquette (2024-2025)

Introduction: A Cultural Shade of Oaxaca

Traveling to Oaxaca is a cultural voyage as well as a physical one. It is essential to comprehend local etiquette and suggestions in order to guarantee a smooth and engaging trip. All woven into the colorful weaves of Oaxacan life, this in-depth book will help you understand the nuances of cultural etiquette, offer crucial safety advice, and encourage responsible tourism practices.

Cultural Etiquette: Navigating Social Norms with Grace

Greetings and Politeness

Accept the friendliness of Oaxacan culture by learning appropriate greetings. It is traditional to shake hands and say "Buenos días" (good morning), "Buenas tardes" (good afternoon), or "Buenas noches" (good evening) in a cordial manner. It's polite to say "buen provecho" (enjoy your supper) to people as you enter stores or small businesses.

Respecting Personal Space

Even though Oaxacans are often amiable and social, it's important to respect people's personal space. It's best to keep your distance during chats, especially if you've just met someone. This thoughtfulness promotes a constructive dialogue and is consistent with the cultural emphasis on respect for one another.

Photography Etiquette

Photographers find Oaxaca to be a refuge, but it's important to get permission before shooting anyone's picture, especially in indigenous areas. Some residents could object to being photographed for private or cultural reasons. Respect their requests at all times, and talk to them before taking a candid photo.

Traditional Customs in Indigenous Communities

Learn about the unique practices of indigenous tribes if you intend to visit them. For instance, it's common practice to inquire about photographic permission in many Zapotec and Mixtec villages, and occasionally a little payment may be requested in exchange. Engage in community events with a humble attitude and an open mind.

Safety Tips: Navigating Oaxaca Securely

Secure Handling of Valuables

Although Oaxaca is regarded for its safe atmosphere, you should always use caution when handling your possessions. Use anti-theft bags, lock up your valuables, and pay attention to your surroundings—especially in crowded places. Steer clear of showcasing pricey goods, and for extra precaution, think about wearing a money belt.

Navigation in Urban Areas

Watch out for pedestrian signals and traffic laws when you stroll Oaxaca's colorful streets. When crossing the street, use the designated crosswalks and pay attention to oncoming traffic. Although most Oaxacan drivers are courteous, it is nevertheless advisable to drive carefully, particularly in crowded cities.

Health and Hygiene Practices

Put your health first by wearing sunscreen, drinking enough of water, and maintaining proper cleanliness. Because of Oaxaca's sometimes heated weather, bring a reusable water bottle and don't forget to wear sunscreen. Always wash your hands before eating, and keep hand sanitizer on hand in case soap and water aren't easily accessible.

Emergency Contacts and Local Assistance

Learn the location of the closest medical facilities and emergency contact numbers. In Mexico, the emergency number is 911. Maintain a contact list that includes the embassy or consulate of your nation. Don't be afraid to ask for assistance or instructions if you need those locals are usually happy to help.

Responsible Tourism Practices: Nurturing Cultural Exchange

Sustainable Transportation Choices

To lessen your impact on the environment, choose environmentally friendly modes of transportation. In the heart of Oaxaca, explore the city by bicycle or on foot. If you're going somewhere farther away, think about using public transit or more environmentally friendly options. Reduce the amount of single-use plastics and help to protect Oaxaca's natural beauty.

Support Local Artisans and Businesses

Accept responsible tourism by patronizing regional companies and artists. If you buy mementos from local vendors or craftspeople, you may be sure that your money is helping the neighborhood. Select fair-trade and environmentally friendly goods that enhance the livelihoods of regional producers and advance sustainable travel.

Cultural Sensitivity in Religious Sites

Be mindful of other cultures when you visit places of worship, such as cathedrals and churches. Avoid having loud talks and dress modestly, covering your legs and shoulders. Observe any established guidelines or rules. When participating in religious ceremonies, keep silent and try not to disturb the aura of sacredness.

Waste Reduction Practices

Reduce your waste to help keep Oaxaca clean. Don't use single-use plastics, carry a reusable water bottle, and dispose of your litter correctly. If there are opportunities, take part in community cleanup campaigns. Adopting conscientious trash reduction techniques makes you a champion for Oaxaca's sustainable tourism industry.

Integration into Oaxacan Life: Embracing the Local Spirit

Language Appreciation

Even though many people in the popular tourist districts of Oaxaca know English, it is still appreciated if you can speak a few simple Spanish words. When visitors try to speak with locals in their language, they greet them with warmth. To improve your cross-cultural communication and forge deep connections, become familiar with common phrases, greetings, and expressions.

Participation in Community Events

Participate in cultural events and activities to foster a sense of community within the area. Take part in community events, art exhibits, or festivals to fully experience Oaxacan culture. Your sincere curiosity about regional customs promotes a feeling of solidarity and admiration for the region's diverse cultural heritage.

Culinary Exploration with Respect

Oaxaca is known for its delicious food, and you can have a more satisfying culinary experience if you honor the customs of the locals. Embrace the local ingredients and cooking techniques while keeping an open mind when attempting traditional recipes. When dining at local restaurants or homes, be appreciative of the food and the work that went into each dish.

Conclusion: A Harmonious Journey through Oaxacan Culture

These insider advice and etiquette standards will act as your compass as you set out on your Oaxacan adventure and navigate the region's colorful weaves and subtle cultural differences. Warm Oaxacan greetings should be accepted, caution should be exercised when navigating the streets, and responsible tourism practices that improve the community's well-being should be fostered. By doing this, you elevate yourself from being a mere tourist to a respectful member of Oaxaca's vibrant cultural symphony. ¡Welcome to Oaxaca! (Greetings from Oaxaca!)

Local Insights: Navigating Oaxaca's Rich Cultural Mosaic

Indigenous Languages and Cultural Sensitivity

Numerous indigenous communities, each with its unique language and customs, can be found in Oaxaca. Even though Spanish is a common language in the region, particularly in tourist regions, it is courteous to recognize and value the variety of languages spoken there. Acquiring a few words in the indigenous Zapotec or Mixtec languages of the area shows cultural awareness and strengthens ties to the community.

Understanding Traditional Markets

The marketplaces of Oaxaca are lively centers of activity that provide a sensory extravaganza of flavors, colors, and scents. Remember to haggle politely while you explore historic markets like Mercado Benito Juarez. Although bargaining is a widespread activity, it's important to keep a polite and grateful attitude. The market experience is enhanced by interacting with merchants, enquiring about goods, and demonstrating sincere interest in the regional crafts.

Festivals and Celebrations

Numerous vibrant festivals and celebrations that have their roots in centuries-old customs can be found throughout Oaxaca's calendar. To schedule your visit during events like the Guelaguetza Festival or Day of the Dead celebrations, check the local events calendar. You can take part in happy community celebrations and get an up-close look at Oaxaca's cultural history by attending these events.

Safety Tips for Exploring Oaxaca's Natural Wonders

Eco-Friendly Exploration of Natural Sites

From the Oaxacan coast to Hierve el Agua, Oaxaca is home to breathtaking natural beauties. Follow designated routes, show consideration for wildlife, and don't leave any evidence of your visit when exploring these sites. Select environmentally responsible tour companies who place a high value on conservation, and be aware of the potential effects of your presence on delicate ecosystems.

Weather Preparedness for Outdoor Activities

The varied topography of Oaxaca provides chances for outdoor pursuits like trekking and beach sports. Make checking the weather prediction and packing appropriately your top priority. Keep enough water with you, dress and shoe appropriately, and be conscious of your physical limitations. When participating in outdoor activities under the leadership of knowledgeable local guides, heed their advice.

Respect for Archaeological Sites

Archaeologically significant locations include Monte Albán and Mitla, which are emblematic of past civilizations. Respect the site by following the guidelines, staying off any buildings, and not moving or touching any artifacts. Respectfully admire the historical riches and recognize how crucial it is to preserve these cultural heritage for next generations.

Exploring Oaxaca's Nightlife: A Harmonious Experience

Nightlife Etiquette in Bars and Clubs

The nightlife of Oaxaca is a colorful quilt of performances of traditional music and mezcal. Observe polite conduct in bars and clubs whilst taking in the nightlife. Particularly in residential areas, keep noise levels in check and show consideration for the surrounding neighborhood. In order to maintain harmony and a pleasurable experience for everybody, abide by the establishment's guidelines and respect other customers' privacy.

Transportation Safety After Dark

Oaxaca is generally safe, however while exploring the city after dark, it's best to put transportation safety first. Utilize reliable ride-sharing applications or taxi services, particularly in the evening. When strolling, stay in well-lit places and go in groups. Being aware of your surroundings and maintaining your vigilance will help you have a safe and pleasurable evening.

Culinary Exploration in the Evening

Oaxaca has a thriving nightlife scene for foodies, with a wide selection of delicious street cuisine and late-night restaurants. For a midnight gastronomic exploration, venture into well-lit and popular places. Be mindful of street food hygiene and choose vendors who follow hygienic methods. Ask the locals for advice and enjoy the flavors of the night with a discriminating yet daring palate.

Oaxaca's Warm Farewell: Integrating Cultural Memories

Reflecting on Cultural Encounters

As your time in Oaxaca comes to an end, consider the experiences and cultural interactions you have embraced. Smiles, anecdotes, and seeing the local way of life all weave together to create a weaves of memories that will always be a part of your trip story. Thank the Oaxacan people for the wonderful experience and the connections you formed.

Sustainable Souvenirs and Mementos

When choosing mementos, choose objects that support ethical and sustainable activities. Select goods created by regional artisans to help preserve traditional skills and to support their craft. Eco-friendly mementos that capture the spirit of Oaxaca's rich cultural past include hand-woven fabrics and regionally manufactured crafts.

Cultural Exchange and Continued Learning

Bring the essence of Oaxaca with you when you leave, not only in the form of material mementos but also in the intangible lessons gained and cross-cultural interactions experienced. Keep interacting with Oaxacan culture even though you are far away. You can do this by reading books, attending online events, or staying in touch with friends and acquaintances you met along the way. The relationships you make in Oaxaca can go far beyond its boundaries, bringing the richness of global diversity into your life.

Final Thoughts: A Gracious Departure from Oaxaca

As you say goodbye to Oaxaca with memories of responsible tourism, cultural discovery, and local interactions in tow, keep in mind that travel is more than just getting from one place to another; it's a life-changing experience that will never fade from your memory. I hope that Oaxaca's colorful culture reverberates within of you, reminding you of the harmonious and enriching weaves that was spun during your visit. ¡Fast forward, Oaxaca! (Until our next encounter, Oaxaca!)

Discovering Oaxaca's Enchanting Surroundings: Unveiling Day Trips and Excursions (2024-2025)

Introduction: Beyond Oaxaca City's Borders

Don't limit your exploration of Oaxaca to the city center as you go further into its colorful fabric. There are many charming towns and outdoor activities in the area that are just waiting to be explored. This extensive book highlights the natural beauty of Oaxaca's environs and offers a variety of day trips and excursions that guarantee amazing experiences, cultural immersion, and breathtaking scenery.

Explore Nearby Villages: Cultural Gems Awaiting Discovery

Teotitlán del Valle: The Weaver's Haven

Visit the community of Teotitlan del Valle, which is recognized for its extensive textile traditions. This hamlet, which is home to talented weavers, provides an insight into the complex process of making colorful rugs and fabrics. Check out the local studios where craftspeople use generations-old Zapotec skills. Talk to weavers, see how to dye natural fabrics, and maybe take home a one-of-a-kind handmade cloth as a permanent souvenir of your trip.

Address: Teotitlán del Valle, Oaxaca, Mexico
Latitude: 17.0554° N

Longitude: 96.5616° W

Hierve el Agua: Nature's Infinity Pools

Travel to Hierve el Agua, a natural beauty that resembles gushing waterfalls that have been frozen in time. Actually, these "petrified waterfalls" are mineral-rich springs that have been producing breathtaking terraces for millennia. Savor the tranquility of this unusual geological structure, take a refreshing plunge in the natural pools, and gaze at the expansive vistas of the Oaxacan landscape.

Address: Hierve el Agua, San Isidro Roaguía, Oaxaca, Mexico
Latitude: 17.2541° N
Longitude: 97.2153° W

San Martín Tilcajete: Whimsical Alebrijes

Enter the world of alebrijes, fanciful, brightly colored folk art sculptures from Mexico. San Martín Tilcajete is widely recognized for its alebrije workshops, where talented craftspeople create unique animals out of wood. Take in the elaborate painting techniques that give life to these fascinating creatures as you stroll through the streets decked up with these fanciful masterpieces.

Address: San Martín Tilcajete, Oaxaca, Mexico
Latitude: 17.0265° N
Longitude: 96.7251° W

Mitla: Archeological Splendor

Explore the pre-Columbian history of Oaxaca by going to Mitla, an archeological site with striking Zapotec architecture. Discover the elaborate stone mosaics adorning the historic buildings and experience the tangible ties to the area's indigenous heritage. You can experience a deep time travel at the archaeological site, where you can see the creativity and skill of past civilizations.

Address: Mitla, Oaxaca, Mexico

Latitude: 16.9213° N
Longitude: 96.4142° W

Outdoor Adventures: Navigating Nature's Playground

Monte Albán: Ancient City in the Sky

Take a trip back in time to Monte Albán, an old Zapotec city situated atop a sweeping slope. Explore the vast archeological site, which reveals the story of the pre-Columbian civilizations of Oaxaca. Take in the breath-taking views from the top of the Pyramid of the Sun, as well as the elaborate stelae and ball courts that hold secrets about a bygone era.

Address: Monte Albán, Oaxaca, Mexico
Latitude: 17.0430° N
Longitude: 96.7676° W

Sierra Norte: Eco-Tourism Paradise

The Sierra Norte entices nature lovers with its verdant vistas and native populations. Take part in environmentally beneficial activities like hiking and bird watching while breathing in the clean mountain air. A collection of mountain settlements called Pueblos Mancomunados provides sustainable ecotourism activities, such as guided walks and lodging in cabins owned by the community.

Address: Sierra Norte, Oaxaca, Mexico
Latitude: 17.1740° N
Longitude: 96.7827° W

Zipolite and Mazunte: Coastal Retreats

Take a seaside vacation to Zipolite and Mazunte, two charming beach towns on the Pacific coast of Oaxaca. With its bohemian vibe, Zipolite welcomes you to relax on its golden sands and take in the laid-back beach lifestyle. In contrast, Mazunte provides the chance to explore the quaint village and pay a visit to the National Mexican Turtle Center.

Address (Zipolite): Zipolite, Oaxaca, Mexico
Latitude: 15.6561° N
Longitude: 96.4936° W

Address (Mazunte): Mazunte, Oaxaca, Mexico
Latitude: 15.6525° N
Longitude: 96.5465° W

Lagunas de Chacahua: Avian Paradise

Lagunas de Chacahua is an avian paradise for birdwatchers. This biosphere reserve is a birder's paradise with its network of lagoons and mangrove woods. Discover the mangrove ecosystems, cruise the rivers in a boat, and take in the diverse array of birds that live in this coastal haven.

Address: Lagunas de Chacahua, Oaxaca, Mexico
Latitude: 15.8134° N
Longitude: 97.0129° W

Culinary Excursions: Tasting Oaxaca's Gastronomic Heritage

Tlayudas in Zaachila: A Culinary Expedition

Visit Zaachila, a town recognized for its lively markets and, most importantly, its tlayudas, and go on a culinary excursion. Beans, cheese, meats, and avocado make up a savory topping for these big, crunchy tortillas. Savor this Oaxacan gastronomic delight al fresco while perusing the colorful assortment of ingredients at the local market.

Address: Zaachila, Oaxaca, Mexico

Latitude: 16.9175° N
Longitude: 96.7638° W

Mezcal Tasting in Santiago Matatlán: The Mezcal Capital

Visit Santiago Matatlán, known as the "World Capital of Mezcal," and get hands-on experience making mezcal. Go to authentic mezcal distilleries, or palenques, to see how the famous alcohol is made from agave hearts through a complex procedure. Interact with mezcaleros, discover the various kinds, and enjoy the rich, nuanced flavors of this iconic Oaxacan liqueur.

Address: Santiago Matatlán, Oaxaca, Mexico
Latitude: 16.9439° N
Longitude: 96.4499° W

Cultural Immersion: Festivals and Celebrations in Nearby Towns

Guelaguetza Festival in July: A Spectacle of Culture

Schedule your trip for July, when the Guelaguetza Festival takes place—a magnificent celebration of Oaxacan culture. See vivid parades, colorful costumes, and traditional dances by traveling to the towns of Tlacolula or Zaachila. The Guelaguetza, which translates to "offering" in Zapotec, is a stunning exhibition of folklore and custom that highlights the richness and diversity of Oaxaca's indigenous populations.

Addresses: Zaachila, Oaxaca, Mexico (Alternate: Tlacolula, Oaxaca, Mexico)
Latitude: 16.9175° N (Zaachila) / 16.0609° N (Tlacolula)
Longitude: 96.7638° W (Zaachila) / 96.4661° W (Tlacolula)

Day of the Dead in Xoxocotlán: A Timeless Tradition

Discover the enchantment of Day of the Dead festivities in Xoxocotlán, a community where colorful processions and ingrained customs bring this ancient custom to life. Admire ornately adorned altars, participate with the community in paying tribute to lost loved ones, and take in the mesmerizing lighted vigils that provide a moving and unforgettable experience.

Address: Xoxocotlán, Oaxaca, Mexico
Latitude: 17.0300° N
Longitude: 96.6806° W

Planning Your Excursions: Practical Tips for Seamless Exploration

Transportation Options

Take into account a variety of transportation options while organizing day trips. You can be flexible and travel at your own speed when you rent a car. For easy access to particular locations, there are also private drivers, guided tours, and local buses. Examine the lengths and topography of the trips you have selected to find the best form of transportation.

Local Guides and Tours

To make the most of your day outings, hire local guides or sign up for scheduled tours. Skilled tour leaders offer insightful commentary on the historical background and cultural significance of every location. To guarantee a thorough and enriching experience, they also use less-traveled routes. Look up trustworthy tour companies online or ask your lodging for suggestions.

Weather Considerations

The temperature in Oaxaca changes, making some expeditions unsuitable at different times of the year. Examine the weather forecast for the dates and locations you have selected. Always be ready with the right attire and equipment, especially for outdoor activities. To ensure a comfortable and enjoyable exploration of Oaxaca's different landscapes, check the weather forecast.

Cultural Sensitivity in Villages

Exercise cultural sensitivity when visiting neighboring villages. Be mindful of regional traditions and customs, obtain consent before taking pictures, and interact with the community in a polite way. Expressing gratitude for an artisan's work encourages healthy interactions, and buying directly from them benefits local economies.

Conclusion: Crafting Memories Beyond City Limits

Day tours and excursions outside of Oaxaca City open doors to a world of rich cultural diversity, breathtaking scenery, and engaging experiences. Every experience enhances our comprehension of Oaxaca's complex identity, from the outdoor experiences in Sierra Norte to the artisanal communities with their age-old crafts. I hope your travels through the heart of Oaxaca's surroundings result in moments of wonder, exploration, and creating lifelong memories. ¡Buena exploración! (Happy traveling!)

Crafting Authentic Experiences: Further Exploration and Recommendations

San Agustín Etla: Artistic Retreat

San Agustín Etla, tucked away in the verdant Etla Valley, appeals with its artistic elegance. Discover the old textile plant that now serves as the Centro de las Artes de San Agustín (CASA), a cultural center. Take in the stunningly designed gardens, go to workshops, and view exhibitions of contemporary art. San Agustín Etla offers a calm haven where nature and art coexist together.

Address: San Agustín Etla, Oaxaca, Mexico
Latitude: 17.2717° N
Longitude: 96.7516° W

El Tule: Ancient Tree of Life

Take a quick trip to El Tule to see the breathtaking Árbol del Tule, one of the world's most magnificent trees. With an estimated age of more than 2,000 years, this ancient Montezuma cypress has a girth that surpasses that of the largest sequoias. Admire this natural monument's overwhelming magnificence and stroll around the little village that surrounds it.

Address: El Tule, Oaxaca, Mexico
Latitude: 17.0586° N
Longitude: 96.7210° W

Santa María del Tule: Artisanal Market

Incorporate an excursion of Santa María del Tule, a village recognized for its lively artisanal market, into your trip to El Tule. Explore an abundance of traditional Oaxacan goods, such as ceramics, textiles, and alebrijes. Talk to regional artists, discover how they create, and purchase one-of-a-kind handcrafted mementos that perfectly capture the essence of Oaxacan craftsmanship.

Address: Santa María del Tule, Oaxaca, Mexico
Latitude: 17.0431° N
Longitude: 96.7216° W

La Compañía: Baroque Brilliance

Explore the stunning La Compañía building in Jalatlaco, a district southeast of Oaxaca City. It's an architectural gem. This 16th-century baroque church, with its elaborate façade and internal decoration, is a testament to the skill of Oaxacan artisans. Enjoy the local flavor and historical beauty of Jalatlaco by taking a leisurely stroll around its cobblestone streets. This region has been maintained.

Address: La Compañía, Calle de M. Bravo, Jalatlaco, Oaxaca, Mexico
Latitude: 17.0593° N
Longitude: 96.7145° W

Culinary Day Trips: Gastronomic Expeditions

Tlacolula: Market Extravaganza

Take a gourmet day excursion to Tlacolula, which has one of the biggest and liveliest marketplaces in Oaxaca. Enjoy the sensory extravaganza as you make your way around booths filled with regional cheeses, fresh produce, spices, and freshly baked tortillas. Savor local delicacies like tlayudas, tasajo, and chapulines (grasshoppers) as you take in this vibrant market town's energy.

Address: Tlacolula, Oaxaca, Mexico
Latitude: 16.0609° N
Longitude: 96.4661° W

San Martín Tilcajete: Mole Workshops

Explore San Martín Tilcajete's rich culinary legacy in addition to its alebrijes by going on a gastronomic adventure. Take part in mole workshops, where people from Oaxaca share their recipes for the region's famous sauces. Discover the complex fusion of chocolate, chiles, and spices that makes up mole, then enjoy the results of your work over a shared dinner.

Address: San Martín Tilcajete, Oaxaca, Mexico
Latitude: 17.0265° N
Longitude: 96.7251° W

Photography Day Trips: Capturing Oaxaca's Essence

Sunrise at Monte Albán: Ancient Splendor in Dawn's Light

Set off on a day trip to Monte Albán with a photography objective to capture the historic grandeur of this archaeological monument bathed in the bright hues of dawn. Photographers attempting to capture the enduring beauty of Monte Albán can get a unique perspective thanks to the interplay of light and shadow on the historic buildings and the tranquil morning air.

Address: Monte Albán, Oaxaca, Mexico
Latitude: 17.0430° N
Longitude: 96.7676° W

Sunset at Hierve el Agua: Nature's Palette

Make an afternoon trip to Hierve el Agua to capture the colors of the sunset on camera. The mineral-rich springs and petrified waterfalls are bathed in golden hues as the sun sets, producing an amazing and strange image. Seize the ethereal beauty of this marvel of nature as the colors change and intensify in response to the varying light.

Address: Hierve el Agua, San Isidro Roaguía, Oaxaca, Mexico
Latitude: 17.2541° N
Longitude: 97.2153° W

Crafting Your Itinerary: Practical Tips for Day Trips

Time Management and Prioritization

Make the most use of your time by ranking your locations

according to your preferences and areas of interest. While some day tours can be combined for a thorough experience, others might necessitate additional time for investigation. Arrange your schedule to maximize your travel time and include time for leisurely exploring each place.

Local Events Calendar

To plan your day visits around local festivals, markets, or cultural events, check out the calendar of activities in the area. This improves your experience by providing chances to observe customs, take part in festivities, or savor foods that are associated with particular dates.

Flexibility and Spontaneity

Though it's important to plan ahead, leave room for spontaneity and flexibility when going on day trips. It's common to find serendipitous discoveries when taking detours or seizing spontaneous opportunities. Be willing to change your plans in response to advice from locals or unanticipated treasures you come across while traveling.

Local Transportation Options

For day travels, make use of public buses or shared vans (colectivos) as local modes of transportation. This lessens the impact of your travels on the environment while also offering a genuine experience. For each trip, find out locally which are the most affordable and practical modes of transportation by checking schedules ahead of time.

Conclusion: Crafting Unforgettable Daytime Adventures

Every journey you take on day trips and excursions throughout Oaxaca opens a new chapter of adventure and discovery. Oaxaca's captivating kaleidoscope reaches far beyond its urban boundaries, whether you choose to explore the handicraft communities, go on outdoor activities, or indulge in the varied gastronomic scene. I hope your day trips are full of breathtaking scenery, a diverse range of cultures, and the satisfaction of creating lifelong memories in the center of Oaxaca. ¡Viva la aventura! (May the journey continue!)

Navigating Oaxaca's Seasons: A Comprehensive Guide to Seasonal Travel Considerations

Introduction: Oaxaca's Varied Shades through the Seasons

Traveling to Oaxaca means not only discovering its natural beauty and cultural treasures, but also acclimating to the subtle differences between its many seasons. Every season of the year in Oaxaca offers a different weaves of experiences, from colorful celebrations to outdoor exploration. With its thorough coverage of the ideal travel seasons and weather advice, this book will make sure that your trip to Oaxaca flows in unison with the city's seasonal changes.

Best Time to Visit: Unlocking the Calendar of Oaxacan Delights

High Season: October to March

October to December: Harvest Celebrations and Day of the Dead

The high season in Oaxaca, which is defined by favorable temperatures and lively cultural celebrations, begins in October and lasts until December. The mezcal harvest begins in October, and there are celebrations and festivities honoring this popular Oaxacan beverage. The city comes alive with the recognized Day of the Dead celebrations as October gives way to November. It's one of the most visually spectacular and culturally significant occasions to visit, with elaborate altars, parades, and traditional rituals creating a mesmerizing environment.

Address: Oaxaca City, Oaxaca, Mexico
Latitude: 17.0732° N
Longitude: 96.7266° W

December: Christmas and Posadas

December brings Christmas festivities and Posadas, a set of processions that mimic the biblical account of Mary and Joseph's search for a place to stay. There is a happy atmosphere across the city because to the lights and decorations. Even though December draws tourists, the weather is ideal for exploring and the atmosphere is still active.

Address: Oaxaca City, Oaxaca, Mexico
Latitude: 17.0732° N
Longitude: 96.7266° W

January to March: Mild Temperatures and Cultural Events

The months of January through March continue to have pleasant weather with sunny sky and moderate temperatures. This time of year is great for seeing Oaxaca's museums, outdoor attractions, and cultural attractions without the intense heat of summer. During these months, take into consideration going to festivals and cultural activities that highlight the variety of Oaxacan traditions.

Address: Oaxaca City, Oaxaca, Mexico
Latitude: 17.0732° N
Longitude: 96.7266° W

Shoulder Season: April to June

April: Semana Santa and Spring Blooms

Semana Santa, often known as Holy Week, is a Catholic

celebration celebrated in April with processions and activities. This time of year sees a surge in tourism in the city. The landscapes are also adorned with spring blooms, which provide a charming background for exploring. Although April is a popular month to visit, there are usually not too many people there, making for a well-rounded experience.

Address: Oaxaca City, Oaxaca, Mexico
Latitude: 17.0732° N
Longitude: 96.7266° W

May to June: Warm Temperatures and Festivals

May and June are great months to get outside as Oaxaca gets closer to warmer temperatures. Think of going on excursions in the great outdoors, touring the nearby villages, and taking part in regional events that highlight the area's cuisine, music, and visual arts. The shoulder season offers a nice mix of outdoor adventure and cultural events.

Address: Oaxaca City, Oaxaca, Mexico
Latitude: 17.0732° N
Longitude: 96.7266° W

Low Season: July to September

July to September: Rainy Season and Green Landscapes

The rainy season falls during the low season of Oaxaca, which runs from July to September. The countryside turns into verdant landscapes as rainfall becomes more regular, providing a picturesque backdrop. Less tourists visit Oaxaca during this time, making it a more personal opportunity to take in the natural beauty of the area. Because the rain showers are usually brief, mornings are a good time to explore before the afternoon downpour.

Address: Oaxaca City, Oaxaca, Mexico
Latitude: 17.0732° N

Longitude: 96.7266° W

Weather Tips: Navigating Oaxaca's Diverse Climates

Understanding Oaxaca's Microclimates

Because of its varied geography, Oaxaca has several microclimates, which cause fluctuations in the region's temperature and precipitation. Although the city has a moderate climate, it can get warmer in lower elevations and colder in higher elevations. When packing for your trip, take into account the unique microclimates of the places you intend to visit.

Microclimates in Oaxaca:

- **City Center:** Moderate temperatures year-round.
- **Valleys and Lowlands:** Warmer temperatures, especially in summer.
- **Mountainous Areas:** Cooler temperatures, especially at higher elevations.

Packing Essentials for Each Season

High Season (October to March):

- Lightweight clothing for daytime exploration.
- Warmer layers for cooler evenings, especially in December and January.
- Comfortable walking shoes for city tours and outdoor activities.
- Sunscreen and sunglasses for sun protection.

Shoulder Season (April to June):

- Light and breathable clothing for warmer temperatures.

- Rain jacket or poncho for occasional showers, especially in May and June.
- Hat and sunscreen for sun protection during outdoor excursions.

Low Season (July to September):

- Lightweight and moisture-wicking clothing.
- Waterproof gear, including a rain jacket and waterproof shoes.
- Insect repellent for protection against mosquitoes.
- Quick-dry clothing for comfort during brief rain showers.

Adapting to Rainy Season

Oaxaca's rainy season offers cool showers that add to the area's verdant scenery. To maximize your time here during this time:

- **Plan Morning Activities:** Mornings are great for outdoor exploration because they frequently have brighter sky.
- **Flexible Itinerary:** Be ready to modify your plans in response to weather circumstances.
- **Indoor Attractions:** On rainy afternoons, visit galleries, museums, and indoor attractions.
- **Local Insights:** Consult the locals for information on the ideal times to engage in outdoor activities and weather trends.

Beating the Heat in summer

In Oaxaca, summertime can bring warmer temperatures, particularly at lower altitudes. In order to remain cool in the summer:

- **Hydration:** Carry a reusable water bottle and stay hydrated throughout the day.
- **Cooling Accessories:** Consider a portable fan, cooling towel, or wide-brimmed hat for added comfort.

- **Early Morning and Evening Exploration:** Plan outdoor activities during the cooler parts of the day.

Planning Your Seasonal Itinerary: A Harmonious Blend of Experiences

Crafting a High Season Itinerary

Day 1-5 (October to December):

- **Explore Mezcal Culture:** Attend mezcal festivals and visit distilleries.
- **Day of the Dead Celebrations:** Immerse yourself in the vibrant festivities.
- **Cultural Explorations: Go to historical places, art galleries, and museums.**

Day 6-10 (January to March):

- **Outdoor Adventures:** Explore surrounding villages, nature reserves, and archaeological sites.
- **Cuisines:** Indulge in Oaxacan cuisine at local markets and restaurants.
- **Festival Participation:** Attend cultural events and festivals showcasing the region's diversity.

Crafting a Shoulder Season Itinerary

Day 1-5 (April):

- **Semana Santa Observance:** Witness processions and cultural events.
- **Spring Exploration:** Enjoy the blooming landscapes for photography and outdoor activities.
- **Market Excursions:** Visit vibrant markets for local crafts and culinary experiences.

Day 6-10 (May to June):

- **Outdoor Adventures:** Engage in hiking, bird watching, or cultural excursions.
- **Culinary Exploration:** Attend food festivals and explore local gastronomy.
- **Festival Participation:** Join regional festivals celebrating art, music, and traditions.

Crafting a Low Season Itinerary

Day 1-5 (July to September):

- **Lush Landscapes:** Explore the green countryside and mountainous areas.
- **Indoor Cultural Activities:** Visit museums, workshops, and indoor attractions.
- **Community Engagement:** Connect with local communities in a more relaxed setting.

Conclusion: Synchronizing Your Journey with Oaxaca's Rhythms

Knowing the seasonal changes while making travel plans to Oaxaca will help you create a more relaxing and fulfilling vacation. Every season gives a different viewpoint on Oaxaca's complex identity, whether you're drawn to the vibrant culture of high season, the blossoming landscapes of shoulder season, or the lush peacefulness of low season. When you plan your route in accordance with Oaxaca's seasonal cycles, you are setting off on a voyage that is in tune with the pulse of this ecologically diverse and culturally rich region. ¡Happy travels! (Safe travels!)

Additional Seasonal Considerations: Tailoring Your Experience

Festivals and Events Calendar

The schedule of festivals and events in Oaxaca is a major factor in determining how your trip will unfold. Outside of the main festivities, there are specialty events that appeal to different passions, such as music, the arts, and food. Look through the yearly schedule to schedule your visit during times that suit your interests. Oaxaca's vibrant cultural scene guarantees that there's always something interesting going on.

Ecotourism and Outdoor Adventures

There are unique prospects for outdoor enthusiasts and ecotourists in every season. While shoulder and low seasons bring lush flora and moderate temperatures, high season offers bright skies for hiking. Plan your schedule to incorporate things like nature walks, valley exploration, and bird watching at Sierra Norte. Taking in Oaxaca's natural beauty enhances your trip in a rewarding way.

Cultural Experiences with Local Communities

In Oaxacan settlements, the pace of life might change with the seasons. Make the most of this by interacting with residents in a manner appropriate for the time of year. While low season may offer a calmer atmosphere for more personal encounters, high season brings with it lively market activities and celebratory moods. Take part in regional workshops, discover age-old crafts, and experience the friendly hospitality of Oaxaca.

Seasonal Gastronomic Delights

The food scene in Oaxaca varies slightly with the seasons. Seasonal produce is exhibited in local markets, and the availability of ingredients might cause traditional cuisines to change. While low season may focus on heartier comfort foods, high season adds festive cuisine associated with celebrations. Savor the changing seasons, go to food events, and immerse yourself in Oaxaca's always changing culinary landscape.

Special Considerations for Each Season

High Season: Managing Crowds

High season draws more tourists but also provides a bright and lively ambiance. Make sure to properly arrange your schedule so that you can visit recognized sites after-hours. If you want a more personalized experience, think about scheduling guided tours. If you want to avoid the throng, check out lesser-known jewels. Securing your favorite options is facilitated by making reservations in advance for lodging and activities.

Shoulder Season: Flexibility in Planning

There's a balance between good weather and less people during shoulder season. Take advantage of the latitude of this time by acting on impulse and following advice from the community. Take part in outdoor activities during the day and attend cultural events to fully immerse oneself. You can take a more flexible and relaxed approach to your trip to Oaxacan during this season.

Low Season: Embracing Tranquility

The low season is the perfect time for individuals looking for a more laid-back and immersive experience because it invites serenity. Accept the verdant surroundings and take your time exploring. Remember that rain may have an impact on some outdoor activities, so make plans appropriately. A more leisurely investigation of Oaxaca's attractions and closer ties with the local population are made possible by the reduced tourist density.

Conclusion: Crafting a Journey beyond the Seasons

As you set out on your exploration of Oaxaca's seasons, take into account the dynamic interaction of climatic, ecological, and cultural factors. Oaxaca is beautiful not just because of its customs and scenery, but also because of the rhythmic changes that characterize each season. Oaxaca's varied offers guarantee an experience beyond the ordinary, whether you're drawn to the vibrant high season, the picturesque shoulder season, or the serene low season. You can establish a more profound bond with the essence of this remarkable place by planning your visit in accordance with the changing of the seasons and accommodating its subtleties. En todas las estaciones, ¡Viva Oaxaca! (May Oaxaca flourish in all seasons!)

Navigating Oaxaca: Practical Information for Seamless Exploration

Introduction: A Practical Guide to Enhance Your Oaxacan Journey

Traveling to Oaxaca means not only getting lost in its vibrant culture and breathtaking scenery, but also figuring out the logistical details that make the trip go smoothly and pleasurably. This thorough book explores the essential practical information you require, covering everything from figuring out the local currency to navigating the complicated transportation system and resolving any language issues. Equipped with this understanding, you may confidently traverse Oaxaca and optimize your exploration.

Currency and Money Matters: Navigating Oaxaca's Financial Landscape

Mexican Peso (MXN): Oaxaca's Official Currency

The Mexican Peso (MXN) is the official currency of both Oaxaca and the entire nation of Mexico. Even though some urban places could take major credit cards, it's a good idea to carry cash, especially when visiting smaller towns or local markets. Oaxaca City has a large number of ATMs that provide a practical option to withdraw pesos.

Currency Exchange: Where and How

In Oaxaca City, currency exchange facilities are easily accessible, especially in the city center and close to important tourist destinations. Major financial institutions and banks also provide currency exchange services. Prior to completing any transactions, compare rates and fees to make sure you're getting the greatest deal. For emergency needs, it's best to exchange small amounts at the airport or when you arrive, and then look for better rates in the city.

Credit Cards: Usage and Acceptance

In Oaxaca City, most reputable establishments, including hotels and eateries, accept credit cards, particularly Visa and Mastercard. Carrying cash is advisable, nevertheless, especially in rural areas, marketplaces, and smaller businesses where card acceptance may be patchy. To prevent any problems with overseas transactions, let your bank know when you will be traveling, and use caution when using credit cards to avoid fraud.

Budgeting and Costs

Oaxaca is a popular travel destination for a range of budgets since it is recognized for providing exceptional value for money. Your daily spending will be influenced by things like the activities you engage in, the type of lodging you choose, and your food preferences. A mid-range budget may typically pay for lodging, food, travel, and entertainment. Tipping conventions vary by region, but generally speaking, restaurants expect a gratuity of between 10% and 15%.

Language: Bridging Cultural Gaps with Spanish and Indigenous Languages

Spanish: The Dominant Language

The majority of Oaxacans speak Spanish, which is the official language of Mexico. Even while many tourists, particularly in Oaxaca City, understand English to varied degrees, it's still helpful to know a few basic Spanish words. This improves your trip experience and encourages goodwill among locals, who value your attempts to communicate in their language.

Indigenous Languages: Cultural Diversity in Communication

Oaxaca is well known for its rich cultural diversity, which is demonstrated by the number of indigenous communities living there. There are numerous indigenous languages spoken, but Zapotec and Mixtec are the most widely spoken. Locals in more isolated villages might speak their native tongue as their first language. Acquiring a few Zapotec or Mixtec words might be a polite and beneficial approach to establish connections with these cultures.

Language Tips for Travelers

- **Basic Spanish Phrases:** Learn some common words in Spanish for ordering food, giving directions, and greetings. This small effort can make a big difference in how well you can navigate and communicate.
- **Language Apps:** To get better at speaking Spanish both before and during your vacation, think about downloading language learning applications. Convenient options to practice are provided by apps such as Duolingo, Rosetta Stone, and Babbel.
- **Local Pronunciations:** Keep in mind that pronunciations and accents in the area may vary from what you have been taught in formal Spanish classes. Its flexibility guarantees improved comprehension in a variety of linguistic contexts.

Local Transportation: Navigating Oaxaca's Roads and Services

Getting Around Oaxaca City

Walking: Explore at a Leisurely Pace

You can take your time exploring Oaxaca City's colonial streets, lively marketplaces, and cultural sites because the city's historic center is largely walkable. Explore the Santo Domingo Church, stroll around the Zócalo, and meander through the quaint lanes of the Jalatlaco district.

Walking Tips:

- Wear comfortable shoes suitable for uneven cobblestone streets.
- Stay hydrated, especially in warmer weather.
- Use a map or navigation app for guidance.

Taxis: Convenient and Accessible

In Oaxaca City, taxis are a practical form of transportation. They are easily accessible and can be located at designated taxi stands or by hailing one on the street. Make sure the cab is properly and conspicuously identified. Having your destination written down or knowing how to pronounce it in Spanish is helpful, even if many drivers can communicate in basic English.

Taxi Tips:

- Verify the fare before setting out on the trip.

- Tipping is customary but not obligatory.

Bicycle Rentals: Eco-Friendly Exploration

Oaxaca City is becoming more bike-friendly; you may rent bicycles from a number of establishments to explore the city and its environs. You can see the world from a different angle and cover more ground when biking than when walking. Ride defensively and with respect for the law, especially on congested streets.

Biking Tips:

- Wear a helmet for safety.
- Familiarize yourself with local traffic regulations.
- Choose a bike with appropriate features for city terrain.

Exploring Beyond Oaxaca City: Transportation Options

Air Travel: Connecting to Oaxaca

The main entry point to Oaxaca for visitors coming from other regions of Mexico or other locations is the Xoxocotlán International Airport (OAX). Regular flights are available from Oaxaca to major Mexican cities such as Mexico City and Cancún, operated by airlines. The distance between the airport and the city center is about 7 kilometers.

Airport Tips:

- Arrange airport transfers in advance or use authorized taxi services.
- Be aware of baggage policies and restrictions.

Bus Services: Interconnecting Towns and Villages

Oaxaca has an extensive transportation system that links the city to nearby cities and communities. An economical and effective way to get between significant locations is with a long-distance bus. Buses classified as first or second class have different comfort levels; first class buses have air conditioning and bathrooms.

Bus Travel Tips:

- Purchase tickets in advance for popular routes.
- Check bus schedules and departure points at the central bus station.
- Keep valuables secure during bus journeys.

Driving Tips: Flexibility and Independence

You may travel throughout Oaxaca at your own speed and with flexibility if you rent a car. Both in the city center and at the airport are large vehicle rental companies. Be ready for a variety of driving situations, such as steep inclines and narrow highways. The beautiful scenery of Oaxaca makes driving a fun method to find hidden treasures.

Driving Tips:

- Familiarize yourself with local traffic regulations.
- Carry a detailed map or use GPS for navigation.
- Plan for occasional road checkpoints.

Visa and Entry Requirements: Preparing for Your Arrival

Visa Exemptions and Tourist Cards

Many nations' citizens, such as those of the US, Canada, and the EU, do not need a visa for visits lasting up to 180 days. You will receive a tourist card when you arrive, which you must keep with you and turn in when you leave. Make sure the validity of your passport is at least six months beyond the date you plan to depart.

Visa Tips:

- Verify the precise visa requirements according to your country of origin.

- Maintain your tourist card in good condition.

COVID-19 Travel Guidelines

COVID-19 has affected travel worldwide as of the most recent update, and Oaxaca is not an exception. Prior to making travel plans, make sure you are aware of the most recent health and safety alerts, entrance restrictions, and travel advisories. Keep yourself updated about any travel-related special measures, quarantine regulations, and vaccination and testing needs.

\COVID-19 Travel Tips:

- Monitor official sources for updates on travel restrictions.
- Follow health and safety protocols, including mask-wearing and social distancing.
- Have a contingency plan in case of unexpected changes.

Conclusion: Empowering Your Oaxacan Exploration with Practical Wisdom

Equipping yourself with useful knowledge as you get ready for your trip to Oaxaca guarantees a smooth and rewarding experience. This guide gives you the confidence to travel around Oaxaca, from managing linguistic diversity to appreciating the subtleties of cash to accepting a variety of transportation options. It's important to keep an open mind because Oaxaca's appeal frequently stems from chance meetings and unanticipated discoveries. May you have an enjoyable and seamless journey exploring Oaxaca with common sense as your guide. ¡Happy travels! (Safe travels!)

Local Transportation: Further Insights for Effortless Mobility

Getting Around Oaxaca City (Continued)

Public Transportation: Embracing Local Culture

A system of shared vans, called "colectivos," and local buses travels various routes both inside and outside of Oaxaca City. Colectivos provide an authentic local experience and are an affordable option for short distance travel. The numerous bus routes that travel through different districts offer an insight into Oaxaca's daily life.

Public Transportation Tips:

- Be prepared for crowded conditions during peak hours.
- Confirm routes with locals or at designated stops.
- Pay attention to pickpocket risks in crowded spaces.

Rental Scooters: Zipping Through the City

Scooters for hire have gained popularity as a short-distance form of transportation in Oaxaca City in recent years. Scooter rentals via an app are offered by a number of companies, making it simple to get around the city. This is especially useful for traveling to locations that are a little bit beyond than walking distance or for visiting new neighborhoods.

Scooter Rental Tips:

- Follow traffic rules and designated scooter lanes.
- Use smartphone apps for locating and unlocking scooters.
- Be aware of parking regulations to avoid fines.

Exploring Beyond Oaxaca City (Continued)

Regional Air Travel: Accessing Remote Gems

Although Oaxaca City serves as the main center, regional aviation may effectively transport passengers to farther-off locations. Oaxaca is connected to coastal and southern regions by regional airports including Puerto Escondido International Airport (PXM) and Huatulco International Airport (HUX). Regular flights by domestic airlines offer easy access to less-traveled locations and beachside paradises.

Regional Air Travel Tips:

- Check regional flight schedules for optimal planning.
- Confirm transportation options from regional airports to your final destination.

Interconnecting by Combis: Versatile Shared Vans

"combis" or shared vans are flexible and reasonably priced for shorter trips between towns and villages. Combis connect Oaxaca with the neighboring areas via a variety of routes. Both residents and visitors enjoy using these vans because they provide them a chance to interact with the rich cultural diversity of Oaxaca's various areas.

Combi Travel Tips:

- Be prepared for limited seating capacity.
- Confirm departure points and schedules in advance.
- Take in the breathtaking scenery as you go.

Visa and Entry Requirements (Continued)

Entry for Business or Extended Stays

Verify the particular visa requirements for your circumstances if you plan to visit Oaxaca for business purposes or to stay longer than the permitted tourist term. It may be necessary to get business or longer-term visas, and adherence to Mexican immigration laws is crucial. For the most recent information and advice, see the National Institute of Migration's (INM) official website.

Extended Stay Tips:

- Obtain the necessary visa well in advance of your travels.

- Provide all required documentation for visa processing.
- Familiarize yourself with any reporting obligations to the local immigration office.

Health and Travel Insurance: Ensuring Coverage

Having comprehensive health and travel insurance is highly advised for all tourists, even if a visa is not required. Make sure that medical crises, cancelled trips, and other unanticipated circumstances are covered by your insurance. Verify the precise coverage for overseas travel and become familiar with the Oaxaca claim procedures.

Insurance Tips:

- Preserve a hard copy and an electronic copy of your insurance information.

- Know the procedures for seeking medical assistance and reimbursement.
- Consider insurance that covers COVID-19-related expenses.

Conclusion: Navigating Oaxaca with Confidence and Respect

As you go more into the specifics of your trip to Oaxacan, you will have the logistical know-how and cultural awareness to make the most out of your time there. The smooth integration of travel choices, linguistic advice, and monetary considerations weaves a fascinating weaves that enhances your discovery of this dynamic area. May you traverse Oaxaca's streets, marketplaces, and scenery with the assurance that stems from knowledge and the deference that results from accepting the local way of life. ¡Buen viaje y buena suerte! (Best of luck and careful journeys!)

Crafting Unforgettable Journeys: Suggested Itineraries for Oaxaca Exploration

Introduction: Tailoring Your Oaxacan Adventure

Travelers are presented with a plethora of options when they visit Oaxaca, a place rich in cultural diversity, breathtaking natural features, and energetic communities. Creating the ideal itinerary requires tying together historical exploration, delicious food, and experiences with native customs. These recommended itineraries are designed to take you through the highlights of Oaxaca, whether you have a week or are planning a longer visit. This way, you can make sure that your trip aligns with your passions and areas of interest.

One Week in Oaxaca: A Cultural Odyssey

Day 1-2: Embracing Oaxaca City's Heritage

Day 1: Historical City Center

- **Morning: Zócalo and Santo Domingo Church**
  - Begin your journey at the Zócalo, Oaxaca City's main square. Admire the colonial architecture and visit the Santo Domingo Church, a masterpiece of Baroque design.
- **Afternoon: Markets and Cuisine**

- o Explore the bustling markets, including Mercado Benito Juarez and Mercado 20 de Noviembre. Indulge in Oaxacan specialties like tlayudas, mole, and chapulines (grasshoppers).
- **Evening: Ethnobotanical Garden**
  - o Relax at the Ethnobotanical Garden of Oaxaca, showcasing the region's diverse plant life. Attend an evening performance at the nearby cultural center.

Day 2: Art and Museums

- **Morning: Rufino Tamayo Museum**
  - o Begin your day at the Rufino Tamayo Museum of Contemporary Art, housing an impressive collection of Mexican and international art.
- **Afternoon: Oaxacan Textile Museum**
  - o Immerse yourself in Oaxaca's textile traditions at the Oaxacan Textile Museum. Gain insights into the craftsmanship and cultural significance of indigenous textiles.
- **Evening: Oaxacan Folk Art Museum**
  - o Conclude the day at the Oaxacan Folk Art Museum, celebrating the region's diverse folk art traditions.

Day 3-4: Exploring Surrounding Villages

Day 3: Monte Albán and Arrazola

- **Morning: Monte Albán Archaeological Site**
  - o Venture to Monte Albán, an ancient Zapotec city with impressive pyramids and panoramic views. Explore the archaeological site and learn about its historical significance.
- **Afternoon: Arrazola**
  - o Visit Arrazola, known for its colorful alebrijes (wooden sculptures). Witness artisans at work and select unique pieces as souvenirs.
- **Evening: Hierve el Agua Sunset**

- Conclude the day at Hierve el Agua, a petrified waterfall. Enjoy a breathtaking sunset and soak in the mineral-rich pools.

Day 4: Mitla and Teotitlán del Valle

- **Morning: Mitla Archaeological Site**
  - Explore the archaeological site of Mitla, famous for its intricate mosaic fretwork. Discover the Zapotec ruins and gain insights into pre-Columbian civilizations.
- **Afternoon: Teotitlán del Valle**
  - Head to Teotitlán del Valle, a weaving village famous for its handmade rugs. Visit family workshops, witness the traditional weaving process, and acquire authentic textiles.
- **Evening: Cultural Performance in Oaxaca City**
  - Return to Oaxaca City for an evening cultural performance, showcasing traditional dances and music.

Day 5-7: Cuisines and Nature Adventures

Day 5: Cooking Class and Mezcal Tasting

- **Morning: Cooking Class**
  - Immerse yourself in Oaxacan cuisine with a cooking class. Learn to prepare regional dishes and savor the fruits of your culinary efforts.
- **Afternoon: Mezcal Tasting**
  - Set out on a mezcal tasting tour. Visit local distilleries, learn about the mezcal-making process, and savor the diverse flavors of this iconic Oaxacan spirit.
- **Evening: Dinner at a Gastronomic Hub**
  - Enjoy dinner at one of Oaxaca City's gastronomic hubs, sampling dishes that showcase the fusion of traditional and contemporary flavors.

Day 6: Hierve el Agua and Rural Landscapes

- **Morning: Hierve el Agua Morning Visit**
  - o Return to Hierve el Agua for a morning visit. Capture the surreal landscapes in the soft morning light and hike to lesser-explored areas.
- **Afternoon: Hiking in the Valle de Tlacolula**
  - o Explore the rural landscapes of Valle de Tlacolula. Set out on a hiking trail that leads to hidden villages, offering a glimpse into the daily life of Oaxacan communities.
- **Evening: Stargazing Experience**
  - o Conclude the day with a stargazing experience. Oaxaca's clear night skies provide a perfect backdrop for celestial observations.

Day 7: Coastal Escape to Puerto Escondido

- **Morning: Travel to Puerto Escondido**
  - o Head to Puerto Escondido, a picturesque coastal town known for its beautiful beaches. Enjoy a scenic drive or take a short flight.
- **Afternoon: Beach Day**
  - o Spend the afternoon relaxing on the beaches of Puerto Escondido. Whether you're a surfer or prefer sunbathing, the coastal ambiance invites tranquility.
- **Evening: Sunset and Seafood Feast**
  - o Witness a stunning sunset over the Pacific Ocean and indulge in a seafood feast at one of Puerto Escondido's beachfront restaurants.

Extended Stay Recommendations: Diving Deeper into Oaxaca's Essence

Week 2-3: Deepening Cultural Connections

Week 2: Indigenous Communities Immersion

- **Days 1-3: San Bartolo Coyotepec and San Martín Tilcajete**
  - o Immerse yourself in the traditions of San Bartolo Coyotepec, known for its black pottery. Visit workshops and witness artisans creating unique pieces. Continue to San Martín Tilcajete, famous for its whimsical alebrijes. Engage with local artisans and gain insights into the intricate carving and painting processes.
- **Days 4-7: San Pedro Cajonos and San Agustín Etla**
  - o Venture to San Pedro Cajonos, a Zapotec community nestled in the mountains. Participate in community activities, such as traditional dances and agricultural practices. Conclude the week in San Agustín Etla, home to a cultural center and botanical garden. Attend workshops, explore local art installations, and interact with resident artists.

Week 4-5: Nature Retreat and Outdoor Adventures

Week 3: Sierra Norte Eco-Tourism

- **Days 1-3: Benito Juarez and Cuajimoloyas**
  - o Explore the eco-tourism offerings in the Sierra Norte region. Begin in Benito Juarez, a mountain village with hiking trails and bird-watching opportunities. Proceed to Cuajimoloyas, known for its cloud forest and outdoor activities. Engage in guided hikes, zip-lining, and cultural exchanges with local communities.
- **Days 4-7: Latuvi and Lachatao**
  - o Continue your Sierra Norte exploration in Latuvi, a serene village surrounded by lush landscapes. Discover hidden waterfalls, participate in agroecological projects, and experience the simplicity of rural life. Conclude your nature retreat in Lachatao, where you can unwind in the tranquil

ambiance, explore forest trails, and connect with local conservation initiatives.

Week 6-7: Coastal Discovery in Huatulco

Week 4: Beachfront Bliss and Coral Reefs

- **Days 1-3: Tangolunda and Santa Cruz Huatulco**
  - Head to Huatulco, a coastal paradise with nine bays. Begin in Tangolunda, known for its upscale resorts and pristine beaches. Explore Santa Cruz Huatulco, where the relaxed atmosphere invites leisurely beach days and water activities.
- **Days 4-7: La Entrega and Copalita Eco-Archaeological Park**
  - Venture to La Entrega, a bay with turquoise waters perfect for snorkeling. Discover the underwater wonders of coral reefs and marine life. Conclude your coastal exploration at Copalita Eco-Archaeological Park, where you can hike through lush landscapes and explore archaeological ruins overlooking the sea.

Conclusion: A Shade Woven with Oaxacan Memories

Oaxaca welcomes you to explore its varied possibilities, regardless of how long you plan to stay, from one week to several months. These suggested routes are merely guides; the real charm is found in letting your journey unfold naturally and by chance. May you construct a weaves of memories that speaks to the spirit of Oaxaca as you discover historic sites, interact with indigenous cultures, indulge in delectable cuisine, and take in the breathtaking coastline scenery. Tres años de viaje y aventuras inolvidables! (Safe travels and treasured memories!)

Conclusion: Unveiling the Heartbeat of Oaxaca

Recap: A Journey Through Oaxaca's Rich Shades

Now that we are saying goodbye to Oaxaca's colorful landscapes, rich cultural legacy, and kind hospitality, it's time to take stock of the many experiences that have come our way while we have been exploring. Our voyage has been a weaves woven with the threads of ancient civilizations, artistic expression, and cuisines, from the old cobblestone alleys of Oaxaca City to the tranquil mountain villages of the Sierra Norte and the sun-kissed beaches of Huatulco.

The Cultural Mosaic of Oaxaca: A Symphony of Traditions

The cultural weaves of Oaxaca is a symphony of customs that reverberate through its vibrant festivals, artisan workshops, and archaeological sites. We danced with masked artists during Day of the Dead celebrations, lost ourselves in the rhythmic beats of Guelaguetza, and were astounded by the deft artistry of textiles and alebrijes. Every interaction with indigenous groups and regional craftspeople provided a glimpse into Oaxaca's spirit and demonstrated a strong ties to its ancestors.

Culinary Sojourn: A Feast for the Senses

From the savory aromas of mole to the smokey allure of mezcal, our culinary tour to Oaxaca was a feast for the senses. We enrolled in cooking classes to learn the mysteries of Oaxacan cuisine, ventured into colorful markets where fragrances and colors converged, and had unforgettable street food experiences. The many tastes of tamales, tlayudas, and chapulines evolved into tales conveyed through ingredients and recipes that were passed down over the years.

Nature's Bounty: A Symphony of Landscapes

The tremendous diversity of Mexico's landscapes was revealed by Oaxaca's natural attractions, which ranged from the old petrified waterfalls of Hierve el Agua to the idyllic seaside towns of Puerto Escondido and Huatulco. We strolled along immaculate beaches, hiked through cloud forests in the Sierra Norte, and were in awe of the archeological ruins atop Monte Albán. Oaxaca's rich cultural weaves was reflected in the diversity of its topography, which included mountains, valleys, and coasts.

Synchronizing with Seasons: Oaxaca's Ever-Changing Rhythms

We learned about Oaxaca's seasonal patterns and how each one gives the area its own distinct personality. Oaxaca's always shifting fabric made it possible for us to time our travels to coincide with the beat of the place, whether we chose to enjoy the vibrant festivities of the high season, appreciate the blossoming landscapes of the shoulder season, or seek peace and quiet during the low season. Oaxaca's charms revealed new dimensions with every passing season, deepening our knowledge of its complex personality.

Practical Wisdom: Navigating Logistics with Confidence

Our helpful guide gave us the knowledge necessary to successfully negotiate Oaxaca's logistical complexities. We set off on our adventure with confidence, knowing the subtleties of local languages and currencies, researching our alternatives for transportation, and being aware of admission restrictions. Because the logistical aspects were seamlessly integrated into our journey, the practical insights freed us up to concentrate on the true spirit of Oaxaca.

Itineraries: Tailoring Journeys to Personal Tastes

Whether we chose to go on a week-long cultural voyage or opted for a longer stay to really experience Oaxaca, our itineraries functioned as guides for customizing travel experiences. Our pathways led us past historical landmarks, artisan workshops, food excursions, and natural encounters. But the real enchantment of Oaxaca is in the unplanned discovery that happens on a personal basis for every visitor, resulting in a mosaic of recollections.

Farewell: A Grateful Adiós to Oaxaca

We leave Oaxaca with a plethora of memories, including the kindness of the people who shared their stories with us, the laughter resonating in the marketplaces, the colors of traditional clothing, and the smells of street food drifting through the air. Oaxaca has evolved from a travel destination to a chapter in each of our individual stories—a place where history, culture, and the natural world converged to weave an enduring weaves.

Gratitude: A Thank You to Oaxaca and Its People

We are incredibly appreciative of the Oaxacan people for opening their houses to us, sharing their customs, and bringing us into the center of their neighborhoods. We are sincerely grateful to the storytellers who preserve Oaxaca's cultural legacy, the cooks who put love into their food, and the artists who create with enthusiasm. The relationships we developed with the people there enhanced our trip and made Oaxaca feel more like home than just a place we visited.

Closing Thoughts: Oaxaca, A Shade of Timeless Beauty

Oaxaca is a masterwork in the traveler's weaves, woven with strands of natural beauty, cultural richness, and the unwavering spirit of its people. Let us keep the knowledge gained, the tastes enjoyed, and the reverberations of traditional music in our hearts as we say goodbye to this magical place. The weaves of Oaxaca, which blends ancient and modern elements, encourages us to consider the value of diversity, the tenacity of tradition, and the excitement of discovery.

I hope that our travels continue and that the vivid colors of Oaxaca stay ingrained in our minds, serving as a constant reminder of a place where every thread carries a story that melds with our identity. Farewell, Oaxaca! Until our next meeting.

TO GET MORE BOOKS FROM THIS AUTHOR SCAN THIS!!

ABOUT THE AUTHOR

Joy Kim is a skilled wordsmith who is devoted to the craft of narrative. She creates compelling narratives that educate, inspire, and fascinate readers as a result of their intense interest and passion for investigating a wide range of subjects. Her writing demonstrates a dedication to clarity and inventiveness, and their experience ranges widely from literature to science. She embrace the ever-evolving fields of writing travel guides, hiking knowledge and technology in addition to the written word and lots more. She aspires to impart information, pique curiosity, and make challenging concepts understandable to a broad audience as a lifelong student and communicator. She leads readers on a voyage of discovery and comprehension with each work she produce.

Made in United States
North Haven, CT
07 November 2024

59975510R00089